Unstoppable

Find the Power Within

A Practical Approach to Inner Strength and Emotional Clarity

JF Tiger

Copyright © 2025 by JF Tiger

Paperback ISBN: 978-1-0698098-0-3

Ebook ISBN: 978-1-0698098-1-0

All rights reserved. No part of this publication, either writing or images, may be reproduced, distributed, or transmitted in any form or by any means, including photocopying, recording, or other electronic or mechanical methods, without the prior written permission of the publisher, except in the case of brief quotations embodied in critical reviews and certain other noncommercial uses permitted by copyright law.

All attempts have been made to verify the information contained in this book Unstoppable, but the author and publisher do not bear any responsibility for errors or omissions. Any perceived negative connotation of any individual, group, or company is purely unintentional. Furthermore, this book is intended for entertainment only, and as such, any and all responsibility for actions taken by reading this book lies with the reader alone and not with the author or publisher. This book is not intended as medical, legal, or business advice, and the reader alone holds sole responsibility for any consequences of any actions taken after reading this book. Additionally, it is the reader's responsibility alone and not the author's or publisher's to ensure that all applicable laws and regulations for the business practice are adhered to. Any resemblance to places, events, or people is purely coincidental.

Published by JF Tiger Publishing © 2025

Table of Contents

Table of Contents	3
Foreword	7
About the Author	9
Preface	11
1. This Is the Beginning of the Rest of Your Life	13
Embracing Your Emotions	14
Understanding Your State and Its Importance	17
The Heart to Yes Technique	19
Maximizing Benefits for Personal Growth	25
2. Honesty	27
The Importance of Being Honest with Yourself	27
Being Honest with Yourself	28
3. Exploring Your Emotions	33
Emotions and Feelings	34
Techniques for Exploring and Regulating Your Emotions	37
Integrating Emotional Awareness into Your Daily Life	40
Emotions and Memories	41
4. Mindfulness	43
Breathing Meditation	45
First Practice	47
Loving-Kindness Meditation Practice I	49
Loving-Kindness Meditation Practice II	53
Compassion Meditation	56
Impermanence and Non-Attachment Meditation	58
Emotion Meditation	61
Daily Practice and Progress	64
5. Journaling	67
How to Journal	69
6. Somatic Techniques	73

A New Experience: Body Scan	75
Pillow Screaming	79
Pillow Beating	81
Tensing and Releasing	84
Chest Beating	87
Arching Your Back	88
Punching and Kicking	91
Dancing and Shaking	93
Speaking Sensations	96
Getting Motivated	99
Practice as Needed	102
7. Self-Hypnosis	**105**
A Brief History of Hypnosis	105
What is Hypnosis?	109
Self-Hypnosis	111
Finding and Installing Resources	124
Exploring and Changing Your Timeline	130
Healing Your Ego States	145
How Often Should You Practice Self-Hypnosis?	162
8. Visualization++	**169**
Dimmer switch	171
Dress for Success	174
The Transmuting Shape	178
When Should You Use Visualization++?	183
9. Setting Healthy Boundaries	**187**
Why Do You Need Boundaries?	188
How To Set Healthy Boundaries	190
Expect Pushbacks	192
Putting It All Together	195
10. Adopting Useful Beliefs	**197**
Changing Your Beliefs	199
11. Adopting a Useful Identity	**203**

Authenticity Is Key	203
Identity and Values	205
Layers of Identity	207
Trying on Other Identities	208
Becoming the Real You	210
12. Staying Motivated and Long-Term Success	**213**
Coping with Setbacks and Challenges	215
Recap and Staying Connected	217
Final Words	219

Foreword

By Sanet Van Breda, a certified Mindfulness Teacher, Master NLP Practitioner, Life and Executive Business Coach and President of Your Voice TV Network.

This book is more than words on a page, it is a stage for the soul. Just as I provide platforms for voices to shine across the world, this work offers a space for your own brilliance to emerge. It is a ripple of love, joy, and courage, guiding you toward the life you deserve.

Each page invites you to step closer to your authentic self, with tools that nurture growth and transformation. The wisdom here doesn't just inspire, it empowers you to create lasting change, both within and beyond yourself.

What JF Tiger has created is a journey of awakening, one that meets you exactly where you are and gently guides you toward where you long to be. His words carry a rare blend of honesty and compassion, reminding us that growth is not a straight line but a living, breathing process.

Through his guidance, you are invited to explore your identity, your values, and the deeper truths that shape your life.

This book also offers something profoundly practical: tools you can return to again and again, especially in moments when life feels overwhelming or uncertain. JF Tiger doesn't just teach concepts, he gives you practices that ground you, strengthen you, and reconnect you with your purpose. Whether you are navigating boundaries, healing old wounds, or stepping into a new chapter, these teachings become anchors of clarity and courage.

Perhaps most beautifully, this work reminds you that you are not alone. Every chapter carries the energy of someone who has walked through their own fire and emerged with wisdom to share.

JF Tiger writes with the heart of a guide and the soul of a companion, offering a steady hand as you uncover your own brilliance. His book becomes a mirror, reflecting back the strength, resilience, and potential that have always lived within you.

Sanet Van Breda
Your Voice Amplifier
www.selflove4me.com

About the Author

Welcome to this incredible journey. My name is JF Moreau or Jean-François Moreau for people who like a good tongue twister. Thank you for purchasing my book. I wrote this book because my passion is to help people. I needed extra help in my life and I still do. I was born with cerebral palsy or CP for short. It's a neurological disability and it affects people in a wide variety of ways. At birth, it took about ten minutes for me to start breathing. Doctors and specialists wouldn't know until I was five years old what the full impact of CP would be for me. I was two and a half when I spoke my first words. I finally was able to walk at five after a lot of work doing daily physiotherapy and occupational therapy. Just before kindergarten, I developed enough stability to go up and down the stairs. I remember, teachers paired me up with a friend to hold my hand in the staircase. They even installed a seatbelt in the bus so I would not fly off the bench!

Fine motor tasks have always been very difficult for me and sometimes seemed impossible. For example, writing was very difficult. In third grade, I had to learn cursive, which was torture. After a few weeks, they made an exception for me and I went back to writing print, but this was still torture. After ten minutes of writing my tense muscles would be sore, but I persevered. Tying my shoes was impossible (I don't use this word lightly). And don't get me started on drinking a full glass of water. It can get pretty messy!

At school, I was the underdog. I was bullied and I always felt like I had to prove myself. And growing up in the 80s and 90s, I really loved the Rocky movies, it offered me hope and gave me courage. The song "Eye of the Tiger" by Survivor always stuck with me: "rising up to the challenge" was always something that I identified with because it wasn't easy to be different, it wasn't easy to have a hard time doing what everyone else seemed to do pretty easily. And for me, *the tiger represents strength, courage, tenacity and resilience; all characteristics by which I do my best to live.*

As I grew older, some aspects of my life got easier. I got physically stronger which helped in my daily tasks and, as I learned how to use the power of my mind, living a life full of challenges became easier.

With the support of my family and many healthcare professionals, I persevered, developing a tenacity (some might call it stubbornness) that has allowed me to complete two university degrees, have a thriving career in technology, and be a committed father to three children. Besides my degrees in Computer Science, I have completed NLP and hypnosis, meditation, and Reiki training, allowing me to access deeper parts of my mind, body and soul to reach my goals, no matter how ambitious they seem.

Preface

My goal with this book is to share with you the tools and techniques that have helped me build strength, courage, tenacity and resilience, find peace to overcome adversity, and create a fulfilling life. *I believe knowledge is important, but without action, it cannot move; it gets stuck and eventually decays. With action, we learn more, transform our lives, and move from where we are to where we need to be.*

Think of this book as a roadmap to unlock lasting happiness and authentic empowerment in your life. Each section offers a technique or tool and suggests a daily routine. You can decide to read a section every day and do the routine for that day which would take you on a forty-day adventure. Or you can spend multiple days doing the same routine. For maximal impact, I recommend doing one routine each day. This will build consistency and momentum in your life. Spending multiple days applying the same routine will definitely deepen your understanding and practice.

I truly believe every human being has immense potential, and that includes you. Join me on this journey, commit to practicing a daily routine, and you will transform your life.

I believe in you!

1. This Is the Beginning of the Rest of Your Life

I'm thrilled you've chosen to embark on this journey of self-growth. Starting is often the hardest step; it takes courage to decide you want something better for yourself. But the fact that you are reading this tells me you're ready for real change. I believe this book will be life-changing for you. Before we dive deeper, I have two requests for you: **suspend your disbeliefs and commit to the work**. The strategies in this book may seem simple and out of the ordinary, but they have been powerful for me and others. I believe it will help you find strength, courage, and resilience during tough times and make your good times even better.

Reflecting on my past ten years, including depressions, burnouts, and my marriage ending, I realize that each challenge was eased and overcome by using techniques and tools you'll find in this book. These practices provided me with strength and renewed vitality.

The philosophy of this book is to equip you with tools to process and explore past and present emotions, and foster self-awareness, self-love, and self-compassion. This journey will also deepen your understanding and compassion for others, and give you techniques to build a powerful and fulfilling life.

You'll learn how to:

- harness the power of your mind
- discover your true self
- adopt useful beliefs
- let go of limiting beliefs and
- live an authentic life.

This isn't a quick fix; it's a lifelong process of becoming the best version of yourself. Every meaningful transformation starts with being honest about what we feel, our inner state and our current situation. Before we talk about how we can powerfully shift our inner state, let's first look at how to embrace and understand our emotions. Let's start this exciting journey together.

Embracing Your Emotions

If you find yourself in a tough situation right now or are going through a tough time, you came to the right place. You may be carrying emotions that feel heavy, such as sadness, loneliness, or even despair. These feelings are real and not easy to sit with. I won't pretend to know exactly what you're going through. You might also be surrounded by people who don't quite understand what you're going through. I feel for you. And here's the truth: **no matter what you're feeling, no matter the emotions that you have in your mind and your body, they are valid and it's important to look at them, express them, process them and accept them.**

If you happen to be in a good place, this book will help you grow deeper, savor and expand the joy you already have. I will give you tools and techniques to explore yourself, your emotions and build a life where you are fully present. In difficult situations, we want to be present. It's the only true way to validate and accept our emotions, gather resources we need and take action. In good times, we also want to be present so we can enjoy every minute of it.

The resources included in this book will help you live the life you deserve. They have helped me in a fantastic and powerful way. Let me introduce the first helpful tool through a personal story. At work I was informed that my team's project was going to be canceled and that the people I coached every day for the previous two and a half years were going to be reallocated to other teams across the company. I was being transferred too and would have to manage a new group of people in a very different part of the company, on a project I didn't know anything about. Adding to the stress, they told me that they were not quite ready for me so they could not tell me any details of what I'd be doing. Wow! My mental state was already fragile at this point, and this really became the last straw that broke the camel's back for me. But despite my stress level being very high and fearing I was going to lose my job, there was a voice in my head that came on and said: "That's okay! You've seen worse, and at least you're not fired, right? You'll get through this." This mindset can keep us going, but it can also lead to burnout. It's important to notice here that I was a minimizer. The minimizer often says: "Everything's going to be fine." Some of us might do the opposite which would be the maximizer: "Nothing is going my way!" or "Oh, I didn't get that job promotion, I'll never get a job promotion, I have no future in this company. Wait! I have no future in any company. Oh my gosh! I'm going to go broke." Let me tell you, I've been there too. I've been a minimizer and maximizer. Both extremes tend to lead to detrimental results.

Your first daily routine will be to notice whether you tend to be a minimizer or a maximizer. Most of us do a bit of both, but knowing which way you lean can be really helpful. Personally, I tend to be a minimizer. And when I become the maximizer, it's typically because I have been minimizing for too long and I pushed myself to exhaustion. I invite you to check in with yourself and be totally honest, do you identify more with the minimizer or the maximizer? When we become aware that the minimizer or maximizer has come online, the goal is to call in the balancer! **The balancer is the one who's going to let us feel our emotions but won't drag us down to the pit of despair.**

This book is all about giving you techniques and tools to bring your balancer online and help you achieve a balanced and centered life while being able to embrace and go through your emotions in a healthy way. And this will set you up for success in generating new possibilities, new behaviors and becoming more and more yourself and being more and more authentic.

Now that you know about the maximizer and the minimizer, take some time to figure out if you tend to be a minimizer or a maximizer and commit yourself to a more balanced life by being aware, with gentleness, of situations when the minimizer or maximizer appears. Being gentle is very important. When you notice that one or the other comes in, first of all, thank yourself for being aware. Then, with love and kindness, nudge yourself little by little toward the balancer: the one that will let you feel your emotions and speak out your feelings constructively. Over time, this practice will help you choose healthier actions, respond with clarity, and live more authentically. The balancer is not about perfection, it's about presence, compassion, and the courage to keep showing up as yourself.

Daily Routine 1

1. Spend time reflecting on major events of your life and determine if you tend to be a minimizer, or a maximizer.
2. Make a contract with yourself to be more aware of the minimizer and the maximizer and to learn every day how to be more balanced and centered. To do so, simply close your eyes, say to yourself "I am more aware of my thinking. I commit to learning new tools every day and to apply what I learned with gentleness, self-compassion and self-love."

You'll discover later in the book that this type of contract is a form of setting boundaries with yourself and it's important to start practicing now.

Once we've acknowledged our emotions, the next step is recognizing how much power our inner state has. Our state is like the lens through which we see the world and it influences every choice we make.

Understanding Your State and Its Importance

I will give you a quick win by revealing how to change your state rapidly. This knowledge is designed to provide you with significant personal power over your life. While we will explore states and their transformation in detail later in the book, it's crucial now to introduce what a state is and why it holds such importance. A state consists of multiple facets: our emotions, our physiology, and our internal dialogue, whether conscious or unconscious. Together, these elements shape how we experience the world in any given moment.

To bring this to life, let me share a personal story to illustrate the impact of states. Many years ago, I was on a romantic date, during a challenging period in my life. Despite the tough times, I found myself in a good mood as we enjoyed a delightful evening at a remarkable restaurant.

As I prepared to order my meal, I selected the steak frites, a favorite of mine. Because of my physical disability, I have difficulty cutting food, so I asked the server for the meat to be cut into bite-sized pieces before serving the plates. Although this request is typically understood, on that night, the server did not grasp it. After a few rounds of explaining, they addressed my date and told her they couldn't understand me. I felt dismissed, devalued, unseen, and misunderstood. I became angry and frustrated.

These emotions were far from resourceful, particularly in the context of a date. A more resourceful state would have involved feelings of love, being seen, empathy, and feeling understood. Being in a resourceful state is experiencing positive feelings like the ones I just mentioned, embodying a confident posture and cultivating thoughts that help us navigate challenges. Unfortunately, I lacked the tools and awareness at that time to change my state effectively.

This experience underscores why understanding and transforming our state is vital. Depending on the context, certain states can be highly resourceful, while others are less so.

Now that you see the importance of your state, let me give you a practical way to shift it quickly. This is where the Heart to Yes technique comes in. A tool to turn stress into clarity and confidence. Let's dive into the process of state transformation.

The Heart to Yes Technique

I'm excited to share with you a technique that helps shift a stressful state into a more resourceful, centered, or flow-like state. I call this the Heart to Yes technique. This technique is adapted from a method I originally learned from Tony Robbins. The structure is similar to what he teaches, but I've shaped it to fit the context of this journey. It also reflects principles found in coherence-based emotional regulation research, including heart-focused attention and generating uplifting emotions, approaches explored in HeartMath's work. This version is simply my own way of bringing those ideas together.

To show you how powerful this is, find a situation in your life that you find stressful. It can be a current situation or one that will occur in your near future. I invite you to think of that situation as if it were happening now and give it a number from zero to ten, where zero is no stress at all and ten is pulling your hair out. To experience a big shift, choose a stressful situation ranging between seven and ten. Once you find one, shake it off: literally shake your body. Let your body shake, you can also walk around a bit or jump in place.

I invite you to read all the way to the end of this section, including to the Daily Routine 2 and then practice with your eyes closed. Allow yourself to settle into the moment. Let's begin by putting your hands on your heart, an action that grounds you and centers your focus. Start taking slow, calm breaths into your heart, letting each inhale and exhale bring you closer to a sense of peace.

Be thankful for your heart, be grateful that you didn't have to earn it, it was given to you, whether by God, the universe, or the mystery of life itself. Out of many possibilities, you came to existence with this heart. As you breathe deeply into your heart, be grateful for the life you have, be grateful for that heart, it is strong, powerful, a beautiful heart.

As you breathe, remember a moment in your life which can be twenty minutes ago or twenty years ago, a moment you're so grateful for. Perhaps it was the first time you met a dear friend, or the joy of reconnecting after a long time apart. Whatever memory comes to you, let it rise gently, and hold it close as you continue to breathe into your heart. Once you find one, say "yes" and breathe life into that moment, enjoy it thoroughly, fully step into that moment as if you were there. See what you saw, hear what you heard, feel every sensation, embrace that moment into your heart and feel it all over in your body, feel it deep down in your soul. Enjoy that gratitude once again, that joy, that pleasing sensation, pleasing feelings that you had. Make it vivid, clear and colorful, and feel that gratitude into your heart.

As you continue breathing into your heart, find another moment for which you also feel grateful in your life. It can be a small or big thing, bring it to your heart, breathe into it and relive that experience fully. Enjoy it once again. Go through what you went through back then and bring it to the "here and now" and feel how good it felt, and feel good again. Replay that moment in your head and with your body, feel it deep down into your soul, your bones and every part of you.

Now think of a moment when you laughed so hard, stuff came out of your nose. What made you laugh so hard? Think about how it felt to laugh so hard, feel that joy, that sensation of happiness and love. Feel your appreciation for life and bring that all the way to your heart as you breathe in new life into that situation.

Now think of a romantic, sexy moment when you felt so much love, bring that in and just breathe it in and enjoy that moment in your heart, enjoy that sensation, enjoy what you saw, what you heard and immerse yourself fully in that memory, enjoy it and say "yes!"

Now I invite you to take one of your hands and reach out in front of you. Pick and grab one moment when you were so proud of yourself and when you find that moment bring it to your heart physically, grab that moment as if you were grabbing a memory box and bring it to your heart and say "yes." As you say that, feel it with every bone in your body, feel proud of yourself again. See what you saw and enjoy that sensation once again. Be proud and love yourself.

Now, I'd like you to think of yourself in the future. In front of you, you see all the moments of your life. Some have happened already and many haven't yet. There are experiences of joy, love and pride. Grab one and bring it to your heart and say "yes." And as you do so, feel this experience as vividly as possible. Don't worry if you don't have all these memories right away. Even one or two vivid experiences are enough to shift your state. For the next ten seconds, start bringing as many moments as you can, grab them and bring them to your heart. They can be moments from your past or your future and bring them to your heart and say "yes." Keep going one by one. Bring one more in and place both hands on your heart and appreciate this gratitude for a while, breathe deeply and say "yes!"

Stay in that beautiful state. Think of the stressful situation you chose at the beginning of this exercise and complete this sentence:

"In this situation, all I need to do, all I need to focus on, all I need to remember is _____."

Let the answer come to you, don't overthink it, let it come.

Now think of your stressful situation once again and using the same scale that you used earlier, what is the number for that situation now? I bet your number drastically went down.

That is how powerful this technique is.

The beauty of this technique is that you can use it anytime you need to step into a resourceful state and if, when you use it the first time, your number doesn't go down as much as you'd like, you can use that technique multiple times in a row until you get it down to zero. Once you get used to it, you can do this practice for three minutes on your own. I recommend you do it each day at the beginning of your day before you start any activities. You can remember the same experiences every single time or use different ones. It's important that the events you choose bring you feelings of gratitude, love, laughter and pride. The more you make these memories vivid with all your senses, the more effective it will be.

When using the Heart to Yes technique in your daily routine, practice for at least three minutes. When I use it on myself, I start by appreciating my heart and my health. Then, I recall the first hug I gave my mom after coming back from my first summer camp experience. I imagine vividly how comforted and happy I felt. I then visualize multiple hugging moments with family and friends. Next, I am back on stage winning my high school talent show, followed by receiving my university diplomas. I also vividly remember working on college homework with my cousin and laughing so hard. Afterwards, I move to the future, seeing myself speaking in front of many and on talk shows. And I finish with rapidly bringing to mind past and future events and focusing on how amazing they make me feel as I physically bring them to my heart saying **"Yes!"**

Now it's your turn. Here's your second Daily Routine which gives a simple but powerful practice to calm your stress and shift into a state of gratitude and strength.

Daily Routine 2

1. Do the Heart to Yes technique (you can do it more than once) using this step-by-step process.
   - Identify Stress (optional):
     - Think of a stressful situation you're currently facing. Rate the stress level from zero (no stress) to ten (extremely stressful). Choose a situation with a stress level of seven or above.
   - Prepare Your Body (optional):
     - Stand up if possible
     - Shake your body to loosen up.
   - Focus on Your Heart:
     - Place both hands on your heart.
     - Close your eyes and breathe deeply into your heart.
     - Express gratitude for your heart and the life it gives you.
     - Visualize oxygen filling your heart, making it strong and vibrant.
   - Relive Grateful Moments:
     - Think of a past moment you're thankful for, relive it vividly, and say **"yes."**

- Repeat this with two more moments, immersing yourself fully in the feelings of gratitude, love, and joy.
- Recall Proud and Joyful Moments:
  - Extend your right hand and symbolically grab moments of pride, laughter, and excitement, bringing them to your heart and saying **"yes."**
- Future Positive Moments:
  - Imagine future moments of joy, love, and gratitude, and bring them to your heart as well, saying **"yes"** to each.
- Fully Embrace the State:
  - Continue breathing deeply and bring all many positive memories into your heart.
  - Stay in this elevated emotional state, repeating **"yes."**
- Reassess the Stress (optional):
  - Reflect on the stressful situation from Step 1 and complete the sentence: "All I need to remember and focus on, all I need to do in this situation is..."
  - Re-rate your stress level. You will notice a significant decrease.

With these techniques in your toolkit, the question becomes: how do you make the most of them? This final section will show you how to build momentum and lock in your growth by practicing with consistency.

Maximizing Benefits for Personal Growth

To get the most out of this book, I invite you to walk with me through a consistent journey of forty days or more, if you decide to spend multiple days on some routines. Each day builds on the last, creating momentum that transforms your habits, your energy, and your sense of self. By following the journey in the suggested order, you will optimize your learning experience and practice techniques effectively. Trusting this process is key to reaping the maximum benefits for both personal development and skill acquisition.

Choose a specific time each day to engage with the book's material, ensuring that learning becomes a regular part of your routine. I invite you to set a reminder on your phone to stay committed. Regularly practicing techniques like the *Heart to Yes* will fundamentally enhance your progress.

Continuous effort is synonymous with success. What you have already learned and what you will continue to learn in this book is designed to significantly impact your life, especially during challenging times.

I encourage you to share your successes within our community. Connect with us on our community platform (https://members.jftiger.com/); I love hearing about your journey. Building accountability is another powerful tool, engage with friends and talk to them about this book, involve people you trust, and find partners who can progress alongside you. Even if you're at different stages, having accountability companions will greatly enhance your experience.

I want to remind you that it's important to continue following your physician's advice, and any medical treatments and therapy you are currently undergoing. This book serves as an additional pillar of support to guide you toward the best version of yourself.

Let's step into this journey together. I'll walk alongside you, every step of the way. So set your reminders, connect with someone who can support you, and prepare yourself because your path to becoming unstoppable begins right here, right now. Let's do this!

2. Honesty

Honesty isn't just a virtue we show to others, it's a practice we must also bring to ourselves. Let's explore why being honest with ourselves is the cornerstone of real growth.

The Importance of Being Honest with Yourself

Looking back, I wish I had been honest with myself much earlier in life. For years, I avoided truly examining how my disability shaped my daily experiences. I convinced myself that if I just worked harder and pushed through, perseverance would somehow erase the reality of being different. But in doing so, I ignored the unique challenges I faced.

By refusing to acknowledge my reality, I reinforced my sense of being different and bottled up a whirlwind of emotions. I felt deep sadness over my inability to walk like others and moments when my speech wasn't easily understood. For instance, watching other kids ride their bikes, a simple activity that filled them with joy, was a painful reminder of my own limitations. I denied that pain at the time, keeping the sadness to myself.

By denying these truths, I avoided processing the difficult emotions they stirred and the consequences on my well-being were profound. Striving to maintain a facade of normalcy led me to overwork and isolate myself. Regrettably, these actions took a toll on my personal relationships, severely impacting my marriage. **When we lie to ourselves, we fail to live authentically.** These lies, while superficially sustaining us, ultimately lead us to actions and decisions that we do not truly desire. They silently chip away at our health and diminish the joy in our lives, wielding a destructive force that is all too real.

And yet, even in the middle of denial and pain, there is always a way forward. The silver lining is our power to choose honesty. Embarking on a journey of personal truthfulness is challenging, and there are moments when I still grapple with self-deception. This pursuit isn't about perfection but about becoming more authentic with each step. Every small effort at honesty matters.

By engaging with this book, you are already making strides toward greater authenticity. In the next section, we will delve deeper into practical strategies for embracing self-honesty. Together, we will explore the paths to living more truthfully and authentically.

Understanding the importance of honesty is one thing. But the real challenge is living it day by day, in the small choices and inner conversations we have with ourselves.

Being Honest with Yourself

In the chapters ahead, we'll walk together through the process of exploring our emotions and gaining a deeper understanding of where we are in life. I am eager to share with you the techniques that have been invaluable in my own life. However, before we dive in, it's essential that we establish a solid foundation based on radical honesty with ourselves. You'll often hear me emphasize this: being honest with yourself is crucial.

I invite you to make a commitment, one that centers on being truly honest. In my perspective, a commitment represents setting a boundary, specifically with oneself. Boundaries are a concept we'll explore more deeply in a later chapter. By starting to practice this now, setting a contract with ourselves strengthens our commitment to honesty, and later, it will make setting other healthy boundaries even easier.

Think of how you feel when a friend lies to you: betrayed, distant, maybe even resentful. Now imagine living with that dishonesty inside yourself every day. That's what self-deception does. Reflecting on my own life, I ask myself why I spent years deceiving myself about various aspects of my life, especially regarding my disability. The answer, I believe, lies in the lack of better coping mechanisms. **Often, self-deception is an unconscious act.**

The first step toward self-honesty is nurturing awareness. We must recognize when we are lying to ourselves and strive for acceptance. Cultivating awareness enables us to become more alert to self-deception. Having the courage to be honest is pivotal. If you resonate with this message, congratulations, you've mastered the initial step.

The subsequent step involves practicing gentleness, self-compassion, and self-love. Confronting our shadows and demons, those aspects of ourselves we have long ignored, can be challenging. It is vital to treat ourselves with kindness as we navigate these fears and reservations. Don't expect to catch every lie at once. Start by noticing just one area where you tend to minimize or avoid the truth. Awareness grows with practice.

To effectively cope with the truths we uncover, we must equip ourselves with new tools and methodologies. This book will guide you in acquiring these skills. Furthermore, it is essential that we take ownership of what we discover and assume responsibility.

Your presence here is an indicator of your readiness for transformation. In the chapters ahead, you will access incredible techniques designed to enhance your honesty, manage emotions, and facilitate personal growth. This journey of continuous self-improvement is one I believe wholeheartedly in, and I am thrilled to support you along the way.

As we step onto this path together, remember: your commitment to self-honesty is the doorway to becoming the best version of yourself. Begin here, with honesty. Let it be the foundation on which everything else is built.

It's time to put this into practice. Let's begin with a simple but powerful routine that will help you uncover where self-deception may be hiding and replace it with honesty.

Daily Routine 3

1. Begin with the Heart to Yes technique you practiced earlier. Remember: the events you bring to memory can be the same or different each time, what matters is that they are meaningful to you.
2. Spend time reflecting and writing down any lies you've told yourself—big or small. Be gentle with yourself as you do this. **The goal is awareness, not judgment**. Make a contract with yourself to be honest with yourself every day. To do so, simply close your eyes, say to yourself "I am honest with myself, I commit to look at my life as it is and at myself as I am with gentleness,

self-love, and self-compassion. I deserve to be honest with myself."

I believe in your potential. I believe in you. And I'm honored to walk alongside you as you begin this journey.

3. Exploring Your Emotions

In the previous chapter, I concluded by expressing my belief in you. Some of you might question how I can convey this with such sincerity. My confidence is deeply rooted in my unwavering conviction that every individual possesses immense potential and consistently strives to do their best. Are we flawless? Certainly not. However, *our imperfections are precisely why we are here: to learn and grow.*

Believing in ourselves involves acknowledging our efforts, recognizing our capacity for change, affirming our significance, and maintaining faith that we can achieve any goal we set our minds to. Whether you currently possess this self-belief is not as critical as your willingness to cultivate it.

Allow me to share a story that still stirs deep emotions in me; even now, as I write, tears fill my eyes. From Grades 6 to 9, I was profoundly shy and consistently avoided class presentations. Then, in Grade 9, I encountered a teacher whose persistence exceeded my stubborn resistance. She insisted (indeed, demanded) that I give a class presentation, at least to a small group of my peers. At the time, I deeply resented her for pushing me beyond my comfort zone and was filled with dread at the mere thought of standing in front of the class. The prospect terrified me. Nevertheless, I pressed on and delivered the presentation. To my astonishment, I discovered joy in the experience.

Reflecting on this now, I recognize that my teacher's intention was not to complicate my life. She genuinely believed in my potential and saw something in me that I was unable to see myself. Fast-forwarding to today, speaking before large groups has become second nature to me. If you find it challenging to believe in yourself, begin by embracing the belief I hold for you. Allow it to nurture and blossom into a robust sense of self-confidence and self-belief.

Believing in oneself is an ongoing journey. Whether it involves taking incremental steps toward new opportunities or confronting internal doubts, committing to personal growth and self-improvement is essential. Each step forward reinforces our belief system, fortifying our resolve and opening pathways to new possibilities.

Throughout this journey, hold onto this truth: **I believe in you**. Your potential is limitless, and as you cultivate this belief, you are moving steadily toward realizing all that you are capable of achieving. Every sunrise brings a fresh opportunity to strengthen this truth, beginning with trusting in yourself.

Believe in yourself! I believe in you!

Now that we've explored the power of belief, let's take the next step: understanding the emotions and feelings that influence how we experience life each day.

Emotions and Feelings

At times, we may struggle to believe in ourselves, feeling inadequate or ill-equipped to do so. Early in my intentional journey, I often mistakenly disregarded my emotions in pursuit of accomplishing tasks. In doing so, I neglected to revisit and properly address those feelings. For example, on a challenging day when I struggled with self-belief, I would select a technique to temporarily boost my confidence, enabling me to fulfill my responsibilities. Yet, as I mentioned, I wouldn't revisit the underlying emotions afterward.

Over time, this created internal dissonance. Eventually, my body began to protest, highlighting the gap between my outward assurance, myself declaring everything was fine, and my genuine inner state. For me, this manifested as low energy, depression, burnout, and lower back pain, where I carried much of my stress. Ultimately, my body would reach its limit, sidelining me completely for weeks.

It is essential to honor our emotions with compassion and gentleness. We have the option to process, move through, them immediately, provided our circumstances permit. However, life can be demanding, and sometimes we might need to delay the work. Then we can simply commit to addressing these emotions later. For instance, we might choose a technique that helps us navigate the day while promising ourselves to revisit and explore the feeling thoroughly at a more suitable time, utilizing the methods we will discuss later. It is crucial to take time to address our feelings.

Emotions are neither inherently good nor bad; they simply exist. They enrich our lives, providing depth and meaning. Without emotions, our existence would lack love, excitement, and the full spectrum of the human experience. **While we cannot avoid emotions or those experienced by others, we remain responsible for managing our own.** By employing the strategies found in this book, we can safely and effectively experience and process emotions without disrupting our daily responsibilities or personal relationships.

Today's daily routine is to spend two to five minutes looking in the mirror and affirming:

"I matter. My feelings and emotions are valid. I believe in myself, and I am continuously learning and evolving into a better version of myself."

At first, this exercise may feel challenging. For some, mirror work can indeed be daunting, perhaps manageable only for a few seconds or minutes. Approach this task with patience and kindness toward yourself. If facing the mirror initially feels overwhelming, allow yourself to postpone it briefly, committing to return to it later. Gradually work on building your comfort and confidence because you deserve this affirmation and the self-belief it brings. You can start by repeating the affirmation with your eyes closed.

Daily Routine 4

1. Practice the Heart to Yes technique.
2. Spend two to five minutes in front of a mirror or with your eyes closed, and say: "I matter, my feelings and my emotions are valid, I believe in myself and I am continuously learning and evolving into a better version of myself."

Now that we've looked at the importance of addressing our emotions, let's move on to the practical techniques that will help us navigate and regulate them.

Techniques for Exploring and Regulating Your Emotions

In the next five chapters, we will be exploring a series of powerful techniques designed to help us better understand and regulate our emotions. But before introducing these tools, I want to begin with the simplest and most immediate one.

Earlier, I mentioned the importance of acknowledging and accepting our emotions as they arise, even when we don't have the time or space to explore them deeply in the moment. So how exactly do we do that?

It begins with a deceptively simple action: **we name the emotion.**

When an emotion surfaces, we pause and identify it with words. That's it. We name it.

Let me offer an example. Imagine I'm at a restaurant with my date and begin feeling angry and frustrated. At that moment, I could pause, perhaps stepping away to the restroom or just take a breath and say to myself, either aloud or silently: "I feel unseen. I feel frustrated. I feel angry. I feel disrespected."

When we name our feelings, we begin to acknowledge them. That act alone can start to ease the weight they carry and gently shift our emotional state.

And when we pair this naming with intentional breathing, slow, calm breaths that bring us back to the present, the effect becomes even more powerful. Together, these practices create space for healing, clarity, and peace.

So the first and simplest tool is this: name it. And when possible, combine it with mindful breathing.

Now, I understand that sometimes we may not have the words for what we are feeling. I've been there and I still experience that from time to time. When that happens, it is helpful to have a list of emotions in front of us. The Wheel of Emotions by Robert Plutchik and the Feeling Wheel by Gloria Willcox are great visual guides that expand our emotional vocabulary and help us find words for complex feelings. I even bought pillow cases printed with the wheel, just so I could keep them visible around my home and deepen my emotional awareness.

"Emotions Wheel" (https://glenntrigg.net/emotions-wheel/) by Glenn Trigg is licensed under CC BY 4.0 (https://creativecommons.org/licenses/by/4.0/) / Background elements removed.

I encourage you to explore this tool, you can easily find it online. It's a valuable resource for helping you build the language of emotional self-awareness.

With that foundation in place, let me give you a brief overview of the techniques we'll be exploring in the upcoming chapters:

- **Mindfulness**: A versatile and accessible practice. Just five to ten minutes a day can profoundly change your life. It certainly changed mine.
- **Journaling**: This has been a significant tool for me and one I've found challenging to practice consistently. Yet when I do commit to it, journaling has allowed me to explore emotions, shadows, and inner struggles with depth and honesty.
- **Somatic Techniques**: These can feel raw and even uncomfortable at first. They invite us into the body in a primal way and help develop vulnerability and embodied awareness. With time, they also become enjoyable and even fun.
- **Self-Hypnosis**: One of the first tools I discovered on my personal journey. We'll explore how this practice can deeply influence the subconscious mind and reshape inner narratives.
- **Visualization++**: A group of enhanced visualization techniques designed to change our state and rewire neural pathways. This is more than just mood management, it's about transforming how we perceive past experiences, the present and how we imagine future ones. These experiences shape our reality, and through visualization++, we can reshape them intentionally.

These tools are powerful on their own, but their real impact comes when we integrate them into our daily life. Let's explore how to make emotional awareness part of our everyday routine.

Integrating Emotional Awareness into Your Daily Life

Each of these methods will help you regulate your emotions, process and accept them, and transform the way you think, ultimately supporting your evolution into a better version of yourself.

As you go through your day, begin paying attention to the emotions that arise. When you notice a feeling surfacing, pause and **name it**. If you struggle to identify the emotion, refer to the Emotions Wheel to help articulate your experience. Then observe how you feel afterward.

I first learned this practice during a software engineering and IT conference in Las Vegas, of all places, where the focus wasn't just on technology, but also on team building and emotional intelligence. One of the most memorable lessons from that event was exactly this: *simply naming our feelings decreases their emotional charge.*

I practiced it that week, and the results were profound. This tool is incredibly simple, yet remarkably powerful.

So let's begin today. Name what you feel and notice the shift.

Emotions and Memories

Before we move into the next chapter, I want to offer one more tip that pairs beautifully with the practice of naming our emotions.

As I've shared earlier, my marriage ended and this life-changing event brought with it an overwhelming wave of emotions. In the weeks and months that followed, I felt like I circled the entire Emotions Wheel multiple times. The feelings didn't come all at once; they surfaced unexpectedly, often triggered by memories.

I remember being out one day when a song started playing in the background. That song was tied to a beautiful memory I had with my ex-partner. And just like that, sadness washed over me. Even now, as I write this, I feel that emotion rising again. I can say it plainly: I feel sad. I feel disappointed that the relationship didn't work out.

That simple step of naming the feeling was so powerful in itself. It reminded me that awareness alone is often the first step toward healing. But in moments like that, it also helps to take it a step further: **to recognize that the emotion is being activated by a memory**. That memory belongs to the past. The sadness I feel isn't necessarily about the present; it's about what I once had but no longer do.

Acknowledging that connection helped me gain clarity. I wasn't sad just because of the song, I was sad because that song reminded me of something meaningful that is now gone. And while that hurts, it also opens up the opportunity for gratitude. I can reflect on that moment and say: That was a beautiful time. I'm grateful that I once shared it with someone I loved.

The loss is real and so is the emotion. I feel it. I name it. I sit with it. And I accept that it comes from a memory that no longer reflects my current reality. In doing so, I gain a little more freedom, a little more space to breathe and begin to heal.

I hope this reflection offers some guidance. This kind of awareness, connecting our emotions to the memories that evoke them, can be a tremendous asset. When paired with the simple act of naming our feelings, it gives us a deeper understanding of what we're experiencing and why.

This practice has helped me accept the complexity of grief, allowing space for both sadness over what was lost and appreciation for what was once beautiful. It didn't erase the pain, but it made it more manageable. And step by step, it helped me move forward.

Daily Routine 5

1. Do the Heart to Yes technique.
2. Be intentional and look for emotions coming up during the day and name them. Name at least ten and use the Emotions Wheel to help you.
3. Notice when the emotions come from a memory.
4. Name your feeling and reflect on where it comes from.

In the next chapter, we will discover how to incorporate another fundamental tool into our daily routine.

4. Mindfulness

I was first introduced to mindfulness during my first experience with depression. At the time, I was judgmental and skeptical, uncertain how mindfulness could truly help. I even worried it might conflict with my religious beliefs.

But when my marriage began to unravel and life became increasingly difficult, I returned to mindfulness and began exploring it more deeply. It was during this period of emotional hardship that I began to understand its value.

I introduce mindfulness as the first set of techniques in this book because it provides the foundation we need to explore our thoughts and emotions. *Mindfulness helps us restore the capacity to create space between our emotional triggers and our reactions. That space is essential for developing emotional regulation and inner peace.*

For a long time, I misunderstood what mindfulness and meditation were meant to offer. I thought meditation itself would always feel peaceful. In reality, it can sometimes be uncomfortable, restless, or even frustrating. The true benefit shows up outside the practice itself: *mindfulness gradually infuses peace into the rest of daily life.*

At its core, mindfulness means being fully aware of the present moment, aware of what we're sensing, feeling, and thinking, and doing so without judgment or interpretation. It's about becoming the observer of our experience: noticing our thoughts, emotions, and bodily sensations as they arise.

Mastering mindfulness is a lifelong journey. But it takes heart. We're not aiming for perfection, **we're aiming for**

consistency. Practicing mindfulness meditation for just five minutes a day can have a powerful impact. I recommend starting with five minutes and gradually increasing to ten. Why ten minutes? Because that seems to be a threshold at which the mind begins to settle into the practice more effectively, making the experience more meaningful and easier to sustain. However, as with all things, the real transformation happens outside the formal meditation itself, in your everyday life.

With regular practice, you'll begin to notice more space between your triggers and your reactions. Things that used to bother you intensely may no longer affect you in the same way. Sometimes, you might not even react at all. And if you do, your response may be gentler, more intentional.

As you begin practicing, remember this essential truth: bring self-love into every session. Leave judgment behind. Approach yourself with compassion and gentleness. **This kindness mindset is vital.**

Over time, as you continue this daily practice, you will not only begin to see meaningful benefits in your life, but the practice itself will also become easier. Some sessions will be difficult (let's be realistic) but others may feel deeply rewarding, even blissful. From my own experience, I can say with certainty: each time I committed to practicing mindfulness daily, whether for five minutes or longer, I experienced significant changes, particularly in how I responded to challenges.

The structure of this chapter is designed to support you: each section begins with an explanation of the practice, followed by a guided experience that you can use to begin applying the tools right away.

We'll start our meditative journey with the breathing meditation.

Breathing Meditation

Breathing meditation is the simplest mindfulness technique introduced in this book. It's deceptively simple, requiring only our breath and our attention. And yet, as you'll quickly discover, maintaining attention can be one of the most challenging parts of the practice.

Begin by finding a comfortable position. This could be standing, sitting, or lying down. Personally, I prefer to lie down. However, if you notice that lying down tends to make you sleepy, sitting upright might be the better option.

I like to begin most of my mindfulness practices by closing my eyes and taking a few deep breaths. I shift my attention inward, directing my awareness to the space just behind my eyes. I rest my focus there briefly, and then move that awareness to the center of my head, still behind the eyes, but now centrally located between the ears. I linger in that internal stillness, simply breathing and being present, focusing on that location with intent.

Once I've taken a few deep breaths, I transition to a natural rhythm of breathing, letting go of control, simply allowing the breath to flow in and out at its own pace.

Traditionally, mindfulness is practiced with the eyes open, softly gazing about five or six feet in front of you. Personally, I prefer to keep my eyes closed, unless I find myself overwhelmed by visual noise, such as images of memories or desires flashing in my mind, or by intrusive thoughts. In those moments, opening my eyes helps reduce mental clutter. The key is to do what feels most comfortable for you.

As you settle into the practice, begin observing your breath. Notice the air as it moves in... and out. Some people choose to focus on the in-breath and out-breath equally. Others place more attention on the exhale. For me, I like to tune into the exact moment the inhale transforms into the exhale and from the exhale to the inhale. That subtle turning point brings me deeper into the present moment and helps me remain grounded in the breath. I encourage you to experiment and find the point of focus that works best for you. I suggest keeping one focal point throughout one practice. The goal is simply to stay present with your breathing.

And then, inevitably, thoughts will come. They always do. This is unavoidable human behavior.

When a thought arises, notice it gently without judgment. Imagine your thoughts as clouds drifting across the sky on a windy day. They pass by, and you let them go. When you become aware of a thought, say to yourself: **"Thinking."**

This small step makes a big difference. For a long time, I didn't include this in my own practice. But once I did, I noticed how powerful it was. Saying **"thinking"** created a clean break between the thought and the return to the breath. It also helped me be less judgmental with myself. It's so easy to spiral into self-criticism: "Why am I thinking so much?" or "I'm terrible at this." But the goal is not to have a blank mind. **The real practice is in gently, patiently returning to the breath, again and again.**

Each time you notice your mind has wandered, simply acknowledge it (say **"thinking"**) and return to your breath. If you do that, you are succeeding in your practice. *This cycle of wandering and returning is the very heart of mindfulness.*

This breathing meditation is, in my experience, both the most challenging and the most rewarding of all the mindfulness techniques. It demands our full attention without the support of mantras, visualizations, or other tools. And yet, it builds remarkable resilience and self-compassion over time.

The key is daily practice. I recommend starting with five to ten minutes each day. The consistency is more important than the duration. Even five minutes, practiced every day, can lead to profound benefits.

In the next section, I'll guide you step by step through your first breathing meditation. Let's practice together.

First Practice

I will guide you through your first breathing meditation. This mindfulness practice invites you to go inward and become present with your breath. It's simple, quiet, and deeply grounding.

The goal of this meditation is not to control your breath, but to observe it, to witness the natural rhythm of your body and mind. As thoughts arise, there is no need to explain them or justify them. Just notice them. Gently say to yourself, **"Thinking,"** and let them drift away like clouds across a windy sky. Then, return your attention to the breath.

Before you begin, set a five- or ten-minute timer and turn off any devices that could distract you. Give yourself this time as a gift, undisturbed, uninterrupted, and entirely yours. Read the entire instructions that follow and then go and practice.

Find a comfortable position, either seated, lying down, or standing if you prefer. Close your eyes and begin to breathe deeply.

Bring your awareness inward. Direct your attention to the space just behind your eyes. Feel the sensation of focusing there. After a few breaths, gently move your awareness to the center of your head—between your ears, behind your eyes—and settle into that internal stillness. Simply breathe and observe.

Now, let your breathing return to a natural rhythm. No need to force or change it. Just notice it. Pay attention to the air as it flows in... and out. You may wish to focus on the breath as a whole, or you might find it helpful to notice the exact moment the inhale turns into the exhale or the reverse. Do what helps you stay grounded in the present moment.

When you realize your attention has wandered, as it certainly will, greet that awareness with compassion. No judgment. No frustration. Just gently acknowledge it, say **"Thinking"** and return to the breath.

After a few minutes of quiet observation or when your timer claims your attention, begin to breathe more deeply again. Slowly bring your awareness to your body and notice your presence in space, the contact of your body with the ground or chair, the sounds around you.

And when you're ready, open your eyes.

Daily Routine 6

1. Do the Heart to Yes technique.
2. Practice breathing meditation (five to ten minutes).

Congratulations! You've completed your first breathing meditation. You showed up, you practiced, and that matters.

Once you've practiced staying present with your breath, the next step is to open your awareness outward. Breathing anchors us in the moment; loving-kindness helps us fill that moment with warmth and compassion for ourselves and others.

Loving-Kindness Meditation Practice I

I grew up in a religious household where prayer, especially prayers for others, was a common part of life. I became deeply familiar with the practice of wishing well for those around me. That is probably the reason I love loving-kindness meditation so much. It takes that same spirit of care and compassion and brings it into a deeply intentional and embodied practice. In fact, it has become one of my personal favorites.

In loving-kindness meditation, we shift our attention from the breath to the act of offering well-wishes for ourselves and for others. We begin with ourselves, which may feel unfamiliar or even self-centered to some. You might ask, "Isn't it selfish to start with me?" My answer is no. For much of my life, I focused on loving others first. I poured out my care and compassion until I was emotionally depleted. It wasn't until I learned to love myself first that I could truly offer authentic love to others.

There are two primary variations of loving-kindness meditation that I've practiced, and both have offered immense value. Let me introduce you to each.

In the first variation, we direct specific well-wishes toward someone (or ourselves), expressing a desire for health, safety, happiness, relaxation, peace, and of course, loving-kindness. The exact words you use are less important than the spirit behind them. The key is to genuinely wish for the wellness of another or yourself with an open heart.

Loving-kindness, at its core, is the practice of nurturing a gentle, compassionate attitude toward ourselves and others. It's about softening our judgment, criticism, or indifference and instead choosing to meet ourselves and the world with warmth. Imagine it as a quiet inner smile that radiates outward; an energy that says, "May you be well, may you be safe, may you be happy." It's not forced or fake; it's a simple act of opening the heart, even if only a little at a time.

This isn't just about repeating words. It's also about feeling those wishes as real and alive in the body. We allow ourselves to experience what it would be like to be surrounded by peace, love, and wellness, and we extend that same feeling to others.

If you find it difficult to connect with the feeling of love in the moment, start by recalling a memory when you felt loved, either giving or receiving. It might be a moment from twenty years ago, or just twenty minutes ago. It could involve a person, an animal, or an object, such as a stuffy. The important thing is to recall that moment vividly. Step into the memory, breathe life into it, and allow that sensation of love to fill you. This step is especially helpful in establishing the emotional foundation of the practice. I've occasionally forgotten to begin this way, and I can tell you: it makes a noticeable difference when we do.

Loving-kindness meditation not only fosters compassion and empathy but also nurtures our own mental and emotional well-being.

Let's get ready for your first loving-kindness meditation. In this meditation, you will say loving-kindness affirmations, first for ourselves and then for a person of our choice. You will repeat those affirmations on your own, in your mind or out loud.

First, set a five or ten minute timer and turn off any device that could distract you. Choose a comfortable place where you can sit or lay down. Before starting the timer, read the following instructions. During the first half of the meditation, use the following affirmations.

- May I be safe
- May I be healthy
- May I be happy
- May I be at ease
- May I be filled with loving-kindness
- May I be peaceful

For the second half, use the following affirmations. Replace "they" by the name of the person to whom you want to send love and kindness.

- May they be safe
- May they be healthy
- May they be happy
- May they be at ease
- May they be filled with loving-kindness
- May they be peaceful

Begin by closing your eyes and take a few deep breaths. Focus your attention and awareness right behind your eyes, feel that sensation, and when you're ready, move that sensation in the center of your head, focus there for a moment and breathe in deeply. And I invite you to remember a memory, a time where you felt loved, a time where you gave love and received love. It can be with a person or an animal. Bring back this memory, relive it and step into it. Breathe life into it once again. Now repeat the first set of affirmations and keep repeating at a comfortable pace until half way through and then switch to the second set with the person of your choice. Don't worry if you spend more time with one set than the other. Follow your intuition and what feels right for you at this moment. Also, if you find yourself struggling to remember the words or the order of the affirmations, it's typical. This practice is not about reciting word for word a spell but to embody loving-kindness. You can use your own words. My only advice is to keep the affirmations short and straightforward. When speaking the affirmations, imagine how it would feel for you and the other person to receive such blessings.

To bring the meditation to a close, breathe more deeply, bring your awareness to each part of your body, and feel your presence where you are, then open your eyes. This is your meditation for today.

Daily Routine 7

1. Do the Heart to Yes technique.
2. Do the loving-kindness meditation practice I (I recommend ten minutes). For the second set of affirmations, choose a person you love deeply.

After learning to send kindness in a simple, heartfelt way, we can go deeper. The second variation builds on the same practice but introduces two life-changing truths: impermanence and non-attachment. These qualities bring even greater freedom to how we love and live.

Loving-Kindness Meditation Practice II

The second variation of loving-kindness meditation is a bit more succinct in its language, but it introduces two profound concepts: impermanence and non-attachment.

Impermanence reminds us that everything in life is always changing. The joy we feel today might not be there tomorrow. The people we hold dear may move away or grow distant. At the same time, the pain or sadness we experience today will also evolve. It might lessen, transform, or even pass completely. Nothing stays the same. *Change is the only constant.*

Non-attachment, on the other hand, is not about detaching or not caring. It's about allowing ourselves to fully experience what is without clinging to it, and without fearing its loss. It means seeing people and situations clearly, for who and what they are, without projecting more onto them or needing them to stay the same. Non-attachment invites us to be in the present moment, without grasping or resisting. When we embrace impermanence and practice non-attachment, we reduce our suffering and create more space for peace.

In this variation, we wish for others to enjoy happiness; not a fleeting, conditional happiness, but one rooted in presence and non-attachment. This is my personal interpretation of loving-kindness, and it has helped me tremendously in my own life.

I remember a time, years ago, when one of my employees caused me considerable distress. Over time, I developed a strong dislike for them, and that feeling began to weigh heavily on me. It didn't just affect our working relationship, it created a kind of prison in my own mind. That resentment occupied precious mental space I desperately wanted to reclaim.

So I brought this person into my loving-kindness practice. I held them in my awareness and wished them peace, joy, and freedom. And slowly, something shifted. My resentment softened. Eventually, I was even able to feel genuine care and compassion toward them again.

That's the power of this practice. It helps us open our hearts, not just to others, but also to ourselves, and in doing so, we set ourselves free.

To practice, we say a short affirmation directed at ourselves and then someone else. The affirmation is as follows.

- May I enjoy happiness and the root of happiness.

And later I invite you to say it for another person using their name.

- May [name] enjoy happiness and the root of happiness.

As we say the words, we bring forth feelings of loving-kindness, wishing for ourselves and others to live fully in the present with non-attachment which is happiness and the root of happiness.

Set a five or ten minute timer and turn off any device that could distract you. Choose a comfortable place where you can sit or lay down. Begin by closing your eyes and take a few deep breaths. Focus your attention and awareness right behind your eyes, feel that sensation, and when you're ready, move that sensation in the center of your head, focus there for a moment and breathe in deeply. And I invite you to remember a memory, a time where you felt loved, a time where you gave love and received love. It can be with a person, an animal, or an object. Bring back this memory, relive it and step into it. Breathe life into it once again. Now repeat the first affirmation and keep repeating at a comfortable pace until half way through and then switch to the second set with the person of your choice. As I said previously, don't worry if you spend more time with one set than the other. Follow your intuition and what feels right for you at this moment. When speaking the affirmations, imagine how it would feel for you and the other person to live in the present moment and be free of suffering, knowing that everything is impermanent.

When ready to complete the meditation, breathe more deeply, bring your awareness to each part of your body, and feel your presence where you are and open your eyes. Practice this meditation as part of your daily routine today.

Daily Routine 8

1. Do the Heart to Yes technique.
2. Do the loving-kindness meditation practice II (I recommend ten minutes). For the second set of affirmations, choose a person you love deeply. As you progress with your practice, you can extend your practice to include people with whom you have hardships.

Loving-kindness is about wishing well for ourselves and others. Compassion meditation takes this one step further by focusing directly on suffering. Here, we learn how to hold pain with presence and offer genuine care for those who are hurting.

Compassion Meditation

Compassion meditation is closely related to loving-kindness meditation, but with a distinct focus. Rather than wishing happiness, peace, and love for others, we focus specifically on their suffering. We hold the intention that they may be free from pain and that whatever they need to find relief, healing, or peace may enter their lives.

In this practice, we begin by visualizing one specific person. As we breathe in, we imagine breathing in their pain. And as we breathe out, we send out the wish that they be freed from suffering and that anything they need to support their healing will come to them.

As with loving-kindness meditation, we start by setting a five- or ten-minute timer and turning off any device that could distract us. Then, find a comfortable position: seated, lying down, or standing. Close your eyes and take a few deep, grounding breaths. Bring your attention inward. Focus your awareness behind your eyes, then slowly move it to the center of your head, between your ears. Rest there. Feel the sensation of being fully present. Breathe deeply.

Then, call to mind a moment in your life when you felt deeply loved. It could be with a person, a pet, or even in a quiet moment alone when you felt whole. Bring that memory to life: relive it, embrace it, and allow the feeling of love to fill you. This sets the emotional foundation for the meditation.

Now, visualize the person you wish to hold in compassion. As you inhale, imagine their pain, whatever struggle or suffering they may be carrying. There's no need to overanalyze or get lost in the details. Just feel the weight of that suffering gently in your heart.

As you exhale, send them your wish: that they be free from suffering. Imagine everything they need—peace, support, love, healing—flowing into their life with each breath out. Repeat this process for several cycles of breath, holding the person with kindness and openness.

Once you've spent time with that individual, expand your awareness to others who may be suffering in the same way. Extend the same intention to them: *May they be free from pain. May they receive what they need to heal.*

You can use imagery to help guide this process. For example, I often imagine a soft, radiant light flowing from my heart to theirs, then spreading outward to all those in similar pain. Choose whatever imagery resonates with you and helps you embody the spirit of compassion.

This practice can last as long as you'd like. But please remember to be gentle with yourself, especially at first. You may find that you don't feel much at all, and that's okay. Or you might feel so deeply that it becomes overwhelming. In that case, it's completely appropriate to pause or switch to a different practice such as loving-kindness for yourself or to a simple breathing meditation.

If this practice is difficult for you, try approaching it little by little. Over time, it can help you step outside of your own experience and strengthen your empathy, compassion, and love for others. It has done so for me in profound ways.

If you're someone who naturally feels others' pain easily, this meditation can be intense. Use it to build resilience—to be present with suffering without being consumed by it. If, on the other hand, you find it challenging to relate to the experiences of others, this practice will help you develop empathy and emotional connection.

Compassion meditation is a powerful tool for developing self-awareness within the context of our relationships with others. It gently opens the heart, grounding us, deepening our connections, and reminding us of our shared humanity.

I invite you to practice this meditation today.

Daily Routine 9

1. Do the Heart to Yes technique.
2. Practice compassion meditation. Start with one person you know who is suffering and expand the practice to everyone who has the same suffering. Above all, remember to be gentle with yourself.

As we extend compassion toward others, it becomes clear that suffering often arises from holding on too tightly. This is where impermanence and non-attachment meditation help, guiding us to meet change with more ease and acceptance.

Impermanence and Non-Attachment Meditation

When I got married, I never imagined that it would end. But when we eventually made the decision to part ways, I was confronted deeply and painfully with the impermanence of life. Intellectually, I think most of us understand that things change. Nothing stays the same forever. And yet, it still hurts to face the reality of death, aging, illness, or the end of a relationship. Even though we know impermanence is a fundamental truth, accepting it and living through it is incredibly difficult.

The meditation I share with you here is one that has helped me not only accept impermanence but also loosen the grip of attachment and expectation. This practice gently guides us to reflect on the ever-changing nature of life and supports us in softening our resistance to that change.

To begin, set a five- or ten-minute timer and turn off any device that could distract you. Find a comfortable position, either seated or lying down. Close your eyes and start to breathe deeply. Bring your awareness behind your eyes, then slowly shift your attention to the center of your head, between your ears. Rest there. Tune everything out and turn inward.

Once grounded, bring to mind a subject to which you feel strongly attached, something you fear losing or don't want to see change. It might be a person, a relationship, your home, your health, or even your children's wellbeing. You may also choose something you're idealizing, an image or hope for how things should be. Let whatever subject arises naturally come into focus.

Now, acknowledge your resistance. Say to yourself, without judgment: "I don't want this to change. I don't want to lose this." Allow that resistance to exist without judgment. Meet it with compassion.

Alternatively, you might focus on something you can't wait to be over, a stressful situation at work, an ongoing disagreement, or a medical procedure you're dreading. In that case, say to yourself: "I accept that I want this to end. I want it to be over and gone." Again, welcome your feelings without trying to fix or suppress them.

Next, gently bring to mind the truth of impermanence: This, too, will pass. Whether it's something you want to hold onto or something you're eager to escape, it will change. It will evolve. Contemplate that truth. Let it sink in.

Now begin to observe your reactions. Notice the thoughts, emotions, and bodily sensations that arise in response to this awareness. Don't try to change them, justify them, or analyze them. Simply notice. As with other meditations in this book, let each experience pass through you like a cloud drifting across the sky on a windy day. Let it come. Let it go.

Continue to breathe and allow yourself space to feel. Let whatever arises move through you: thoughts, sadness, fear, even peace. Accept everything with as much love and patience as you can. You don't need to push away what hurts or cling to what feels good. Just be present. Just observe.

Give yourself love and compassion as you move through this practice, always with gentleness. When you wish to complete the meditation, begin to breathe deeply again. Slowly bring your awareness back to your body, noticing your surroundings, and when you're ready, open your eyes.

This practice has helped me build resilience, especially in the aftermath of my divorce. It helped me accept the end of that chapter and embrace what I still had in my life. It helped me let go of what no longer was and appreciate what is.

Let me be clear: this is not a magic pill. It doesn't erase all emotions or dissolve all suffering, and that's not the goal. The purpose of this meditation is not to repress what we feel, but to create space for those feelings, to explore them, understand them, and allow them to shift naturally in the light of awareness.

Impermanence and non-attachment meditation teaches us that life changes and that much of what happens is beyond our control. By learning to meet change with presence and gentleness, we begin to understand ourselves more deeply. We learn to flow with life instead of resisting it at every turn.

I know this practice will help you too. With time and practice, it will get easier to grasp and accept the reality of impermanence and the freedom offered by non-attachment. You are ready for your daily routine.

Daily Routine 10

1. Do the Heart to Yes technique.
2. Practice impermanence and non-attachment meditation for ten minutes.

Understanding impermanence prepares us to look inward again. In emotion meditation, we explore the feelings within us—sometimes hidden, sometimes loud—and learn to meet them with balance and compassion.

Emotion Meditation

With emotion meditation, we gently shift our awareness toward our emotions. This may sound simple, but in reality, it's not always easy. Sometimes we genuinely don't know how we feel. Other times, we're aware of a surface-level emotion, but underneath it, there are layers, deeper truths and hidden feelings that are waiting to be acknowledged and accepted.

Let me give you a personal example.

I'm very ticklish. Next time you see me, please don't use that against me. My wonderful kids, somehow, love to take advantage of this fact. Most of the time, I have to admit, I feel frustrated when they tickle me and it doesn't feel good at all.

At one point, I decided to explore that frustration through emotion meditation. What I discovered was eye-opening. Beneath the frustration, there was fear. Fear of what? Several things. First, I was afraid they wouldn't stop. Second, I realized I was also afraid I might accidentally hurt them because of my cerebral palsy. My movements can sometimes be unpredictable; I could accidentally jerk my arm and hit them. But the most important thing I uncovered was this: I unconsciously saw them as bullies. Their tickling triggered a fight response from my past bringing up memories of being bullied when I was younger.

Once I understood this connection, it changed my relationship with the experience. I'm not saying I love being tickled now, but I'm much more comfortable with my kids doing it. I can meet the moment with more compassion for them, and for myself.

This is what emotion meditation can offer: the ability to explore what we feel without being overwhelmed by it. In this practice, we're not trying to amplify the emotion, and we're not trying to suppress it either. Instead, we invite in what I call the balancer, the inner presence that allows us to feel deeply while remaining centered. This is how we explore emotions without being pulled down into despair.

As with many practices in this book, we begin by setting a five- or ten-minute timer and turning off any potential distractions. Then, find a comfortable position, either seated or lying down. Close your eyes and bring your awareness behind your eyes. Rest there, then shift that awareness to the center of your head, between your ears. Take several deep breaths, settling into the present moment.

Next, choose a single emotion to explore. I recommend focusing on just one root emotion per practice. It's not a hard rule, feel free to follow where the meditation leads, but beginning with one emotion creates clarity and depth.

Gently ask yourself: "What do I feel? And where do I feel it in my body?" Speak to yourself as you would speak to someone you care about. "Body, where do I feel this frustration?"

Allow the answer to come in its own time. It may arrive as a physical sensation, a thought, or even another emotion. If you feel called to, you can follow that thread. For example, if you begin with frustration and then uncover fear or sadness underneath, you may choose to explore those too.

Think of it like pulling on a thread, gently and patiently letting each layer reveal itself in time. Let the meditation unfold naturally. Give yourself space and time to reflect, and listen to what your body and subconscious are ready to share.

Above all, bring gentleness, love, and compassion to this practice. That cannot be overstated. Emotion meditation can be challenging, especially when working with deep or long-buried feelings. You might not get as far as you'd like in your first or even your second session, and that's completely okay.

When I was younger, I felt many emotions, like fear, when my mother left me in the care of someone else or anxiety about going to school. But there were other emotions I didn't allow myself to feel, especially around my cerebral palsy. I didn't let myself fully grieve not being able to ride a bike as a kid or the loss I felt when I couldn't drive at sixteen like my peers. Those were harder emotions, and I buried them for years.

Some emotions take time to surface. Others may come quickly. Every person is different, and every emotion is different. So please, give yourself grace. Let the process unfold in its own way, at its own pace. And this is true for any practice we explore together in this book.

Be patient. Be kind. And trust that whatever arises is part of your healing journey.

I invite you to do this meditation today as part of your daily routine. Give yourself the gift of space, a quiet moment to listen, to feel and notice what your emotions may be ready to tell you.

With these practices: breath, kindness, compassion, acceptance, and emotional awareness, you now have a toolkit to bring mindfulness into every corner of life. What matters most is not doing them perfectly, but returning to them daily with gentleness.

Daily Routine 11

1. Do the Heart to Yes technique.
2. Practice emotion meditation for ten minutes.

Daily Practice and Progress

As we conclude this chapter, take a moment to acknowledge your growth. You've already done so much.

You are sharpening your attention. You're living more in the present moment. You're creating more space between your triggers and your reactions, and I would bet that in some cases, you're not even reacting at all anymore. You're developing self-love, self-awareness, self-compassion, and compassion for others. You're building empathy and resilience day by day.

Keep it up.

There may be days when you feel like your progress isn't where you want it to be. Or perhaps you feel like you're struggling more than you should. That's okay. **This isn't about perfection, it's about progress. It's about showing up, even when it's hard.**

I invite you to continue your mindfulness meditation practice every day. Choose one technique, perhaps your favorite or a different one every day, and spend five to ten minutes with it. You don't need to do it perfectly. Just do it consistently.

Each section in this chapter offers you a tool. Use them. Rotate through them. Let them become part of your rhythm. You don't need to go in order. You can revisit the practices that resonate most with you or challenge yourself to engage with the ones you've found difficult.

If you haven't already, consider reaching out to a friend or two to share this journey. Invite them to explore mindfulness with you. Not only will it help them but it will also help you stay accountable. When we talk about what we're learning and practicing, it reinforces our own progress. And it encourages us to stay committed.

This book is not just about learning techniques, it's about practicing them. Integrating them. Living them.

And finally, if you'd like to explore mindfulness further, I highly recommend the work of Pema Chödrön. She is a brilliant and down-to-earth teacher, an ordained Buddhist nun, wise, witty, and incredibly approachable. Her insights have helped countless people navigate the challenges of life with more grace and clarity. If you're curious, look into her books or talks. Her voice may complement your journey in a beautiful way.

You've done amazing work already. Keep going! You're building something powerful, and you're becoming unstoppable.

Now, let's take a look at journaling, a practice that helps us dig deeper into our thoughts and feelings.

5. Journaling

Journaling has become one of the most powerful tools in my life and, ironically, also one of the hardest for me to embrace.

Growing up, I didn't enjoy writing. One of the main reasons was that it was physically difficult for me, especially writing by hand. Thankfully, technology has made that easier. I now type on a keyboard, and voice-to-text has become an incredible ally.

But there was something deeper holding me back: **perfectionism**. This has been a big hurdle in my journaling practice. I carried the belief that everything I wrote needed to be "right" and that it had to sound profound, or structured a certain way, or be something I'd want to reread later. That mindset turned journaling into something intimidating, when it was meant to be liberating.

Why am I sharing this with you? Because you might be carrying similar struggles or assumptions that hold you back from journaling. Once I discovered what journaling is truly about, everything changed.

Journaling isn't about perfectly documenting every event of your day. It's not about having neat handwriting or writing in a specific format. It's not even about being able to reread what you wrote. Journaling is about *self-discovery*. It's about showing up as you are—messy, raw, reflective, honest—and uncovering what lives beneath the surface.

Let me give you an example of how journaling opened a door I didn't even know was closed.

The death of my uncle, a man who was like a second father to me, was a deeply emotional time. There were about three weeks between the day he died and the day of his funeral. I was sad, but I hadn't cried. His passing wasn't unexpected. He went peacefully, and I was grateful he no longer had to suffer.

On the morning of his funeral, I sat down to write a short note in my journal. I intended to share it later with my family. But as soon as I started writing, the tears came. I began to sob. That moment of writing became the gateway to my grief. It allowed me to feel what had been quietly building inside me for weeks. After writing, I turned to the Heart to Yes technique, which helped me stay grounded through what was an emotional and heavy day.

That's the power of journaling.

It helps us **move emotions**, **reveal emotions**, and **discover truths** we didn't realize we were carrying. If you approach journaling as a way to be your most honest, authentic self, you'll begin to see incredible shifts. *Some shifts will feel small, others will feel big but all of them are meaningful. Each one brings you a step closer to your truest self.*

Journaling helps us notice what we often miss in the noise of daily life: buried thoughts, unacknowledged feelings, and quiet wisdom waiting to be heard.

In the next section, I'll walk you through a simple structure you can use for daily journaling. It's something you can return to again and again; something that, if you stay consistent, can have a tremendous impact on your life.

How to Journal

My intention with journaling is simple. I want to keep it accessible, approachable, and consistent. As I've shared before, writing has never been my strongest skill. But here's what I know for certain: if someone like me, who doesn't naturally enjoy writing, can experience profound insight and transformation through journaling, then it's a tool that cannot be ignored.

You don't have to be Yung Pueblo to write meaningful journal entries. And if you haven't heard of him, I encourage you to look him up. His book The Way Forward supported me during one of the most challenging times in my life, especially during my separation and divorce. His words helped validate the emotions I was going through and reminded me that healing takes time and intention.

Let me offer you a simple structure, something that you can adopt exactly as it is, or modify to suit your own flow. The structure has two parts, both equally valuable:

1. **Begin with gratitude.**
   Start each journal entry by writing about what you're thankful for today. Gratitude grounds us and softens the heart, setting the tone for honest self-reflection.
2. **Reflect on difficulties.**
   Next, write about something that was emotionally challenging that day. What made you uncomfortable, triggered you, or stirred up tough emotions? Use your journal as a safe place to process and understand what surfaced.

That's it: gratitude and reflection. Simple, powerful, and enough. You don't need to overthink the format. It doesn't matter what kind of notebook or app you use, or whether your handwriting is neat. The important thing is that you write every day.

If you choose to journal in the morning, write about the previous day. If you journal in the evening, reflect on the day you've just experienced. You can journal while riding the bus, while sipping your coffee, or right before bed. Make it easy. Make it fit your life. The easier it is to start, the more likely it is to become a consistent habit.

If you know that a certain time of day works best for you, such as before dinner, set an alarm. If needed, set multiple alarms to support different parts of your routine. **The point is to build a rhythm that helps you succeed.**

As part of your daily practice, I recommend including three elements: the **Heart to Yes technique**, **mindfulness meditation** (five to ten minutes) and **journaling** (five to ten minutes).

These small, consistent actions are what create lasting change.

You're learning a lot here but learning alone isn't enough. Transformation comes from practice.

There were many times in my life when I knew what I needed to do but I didn't apply it. And I say that not to shame myself, but as a reminder to be honest and gentle with ourselves. Sometimes I feel disappointed about the times I didn't act on what I knew. But when I catch myself in that pattern, I meet it with love and I recommit. *When we put into practice what we know, that is true growth.*

Consistency in your daily routine is one of the most powerful ways to keep growing. So I invite you to do this for yourself. You are worth it.

I believe in you. Believe in yourself.

Daily Routine 12

1. Do the Heart to Yes technique.
2. Practice mindfulness meditation for ten minutes. Pick one of the meditations we explored in Chapter Four. You can stick with the one you prefer and with which you're the most comfortable or challenge yourself and pick a different one.
3. Journal for five to ten minutes. First, write about what you're thankful for. And second, write about a difficult situation that happened today or yesterday: an emotion that was tough to go through or a thought that was or is bothering you.

Here are a few tips for your journaling practice:

- Don't worry about the length or format of your text.
- Be honest with yourself.
- Don't overthink your writing. Let it flow freely, **with no censorship**!
- And, as always, give yourself love, compassion and gentleness.

In the next chapter, we'll use our body and voice to continue processing our thoughts and emotions.

6. Somatic Techniques

In Chapter One, I introduced the concept of states: the combination of our emotions, internal dialogue, and physiology. Of these three components, physiology is often the quickest and most accessible way to influence and change our state.

That's where somatic techniques come in.

Somatic techniques are simple, powerful methods that use movement and voice to help us process emotions. Emotions can often become stuck in our body, lingering as tension, pain, or restlessness. When we use our body intentionally, whether through movement, breath, or sound, we can release those trapped emotions, liberate our energy, and return to balance.

Personally, I rely on somatic techniques in two key ways: through physical training and through ecstatic dance, a free-form dance designed to reconnect with oneself and others.

Within those practices, I apply all the techniques you'll learn in this chapter. But I also use these techniques on their own.

For example, I recently had a difficult phone call that left me feeling depleted. One of my boundaries had been crossed, and I felt a mix of sadness, frustration, and anger. I still had things to do that evening, but I knew I didn't want to ignore or repress how I felt. I wanted to move through it.

Before continuing with my busy schedule, I practiced two techniques I will share with you in this chapter: Punching and Kicking, followed by Back Arching. Within just a few minutes, I felt more centered, emotionally balanced, and mentally clear. I was able to process the situation with more perspective and carry on with my evening. That's the power of moving emotion through the body. Of course, like any physical practice, it's important to approach somatic techniques with care.

Important note:
Before using any somatic technique, please consult with your primary healthcare provider, if you have any medical concerns. These practices involve physical movement and should be done with care and respect for your body's limits.

Let me also take a moment to speak about something that deeply matters to me: community.

When I was going through my separation, I longed for a way to reconnect with myself, with others, and with life. I stumbled upon Ecstatic Dance, and it became one of the most healing spaces I've ever encountered. Moving freely, without judgment, allowed me to express emotions I didn't even know I was carrying. Over time, I developed meaningful friendships within that community. It became a pillar of support, strength, and renewal.

If you already have a strong support network, I encourage you to nurture those relationships. Community is vital to resilience. And if you don't yet have one, consider this your invitation to find one. Whether it's a dance group, a running club, a chess meetup, or a book circle, find one that fits your interests and start showing up. The first few times might feel awkward or uncertain, but trust me: it's worth it. That first step could change everything.

Building community has been vital for me and that is how I discovered somatic practices. So now, let's return to the heart of this chapter: the techniques themselves.

In the pages that follow, you'll learn somatic techniques that involve movement, voice, and physical expression. These are tools for emotional freedom, helping you process what you feel without suppressing or bypassing anything. Instead, we'll express feelings fully and authentically, giving our emotions the outlet they often need.

If you're interested in diving deeper into somatic work, I highly recommend exploring the work of Peter Levine, a pioneer in this field. His books and teachings offer a wealth of knowledge and practices.

A New Experience: Body Scan

In this section, we explore a foundational somatic practice: the body scan. This is a gentle and effective process to reconnect with our body.

If this kind of technique is new to you, it's normal to feel a little self-conscious at first. I remember the first time I was asked to shake during a meditation training. I smiled and said "Usually I try not to shake in public". Being asked to do it on purpose felt strange and vulnerable. It was a stretch for me. And it might be a stretch for you too.

But that's not a bad thing. In fact, it's often a sign of growth. When something challenges you, it means you're learning. You're reaching beyond your comfort zone and that's how transformation happens.

For some people, especially those who have experienced trauma or long periods of stress, it may feel difficult to connect with physical sensations. You might not feel anything at all or only notice numbness. If that's the case, don't worry. Numbness is still a sensation. Bring gentle curiosity to it. Let it be part of your experience.

If you find somatic work especially challenging or overwhelming, you might consider working with a therapist or coach experienced in somatic practices. Having skilled one-on-one support can be incredibly helpful as you deepen your connection to your body.

Let's make today's daily routine a body scan, so you can experience this practice right now. To begin, find a comfortable position, either lying down or seated, and turn off any distraction and read the following instructions before you start your body scan.

Close your eyes and start breathing deeply. Bring your awareness behind your eyes, then slowly shift your attention to the center of your head. Breathe naturally and allow your awareness to rest there.

Now, gently move your attention all the way down to your toes. Begin to scan the body and do so as slowly as you can avoiding judgment or internal dialogue; focus on the sensations.

Feel each toe on your left foot, then your right.

Notice the skin around and between your toes.

Move your attention to your ankles. Sense the left, then the right. Notice the skin, the bones, any tension or ease.

Shift to your calves, first the left and then the right. Explore the skin, the muscle, the front and back of your legs.

Bring awareness to your knees. Explore the front and the back of each one. What sensations are present, warmth, tightness, cold, numbness?

Move up to your thighs, left and then right. Feel the layers: skin, muscle, even the awareness that there's a bone underneath.

From there, shift attention to your genitals and your lower back. What sensations arise in those areas? Simply observe, without judgment.

Bring awareness to your stomach and your chest. Is there openness? Constriction? Heat or cold?

Explore your shoulders, arms, and hands. Notice each finger, the palms, the wrists. Travel up the arms to the armpits, and then to the upper back.

Feel the back of your neck, then the front of your throat. Shift to your head, your scalp, ears, cheeks, nose, eyes, and jaw.

Throughout, stay present with what you feel, whether it's sensation, emotion, or even nothing at all.

Now, imagine a wave of calm flowing down from the top of your head to your toes. Let that wave move through you a few times, from head to toe, with your breath.

Take a moment and ask your body if there's anything it wants you to notice. Pause. Listen. And thank your body for showing up, for holding you, for carrying you.

When you're ready, begin to breathe a little deeper. Slowly open your eyes. And notice your surroundings.

This exercise is your routine for today, fostering a mindful connection with your body. I invite you to return to this practice regularly, as part of your daily routine.

Daily Routine 13

1. Do the Heart to Yes technique.
2. Practice mindfulness meditation for ten minutes.
3. Journal for five to ten minutes.
4. Do the body scan exercise. I recommend taking five to ten minutes.
    - Take the time to scan your entire body. From your toes to the top of your head.
    - Go slowly and pay attention to any sensation.
    - You can also have a dialogue with your body: "What would you like me to notice?"
    - Explore parts of your body you're usually not aware of: your skin, the space behind your knees and your armpits.
    - Thank your body for its functions, for every good and useful service it offers for you.

Once you've tried the gentle practice of a body scan, you may be ready for something more raw and expressive. The next technique, Pillow Screaming, offers exactly that.

Pillow Screaming

Pillow Screaming is simple, powerful, and deeply cathartic.

Why scream into a pillow? First, the pillow helps you avoid alarming your neighbors or anyone else nearby. But more importantly, screaming in a pillow allows us to express intense emotions, especially anger and frustration, in a safe, contained, and physical way.

Let me ask you something: ***Do you think anger is wrong?***

Many of us do. Most of us were taught, directly or indirectly, that anger is bad. As children, when we expressed anger, we were often reprimanded and told to calm down, be quiet, or behave. Over time, we learned to suppress those feelings. But that doesn't mean the anger went away. It just stayed stuck in our bodies.

It's time to return to the basics.

Look at animals. When they feel threatened, they growl, hiss, or roar. They use their voices as signals. Children do this too. The very first thing a baby does when it's unhappy is scream. Teenagers scream, too. It's one of the most natural human expressions of distress.

Anger is not bad. It's not good, either. It's just a feeling. It is neutral. Let me clear though: screaming at someone is usually unhelpful, unless your goal is to drive them away. In this practice, we don't scream at anyone; it is useful as it gives us a safe outlet to move and process our stuck emotions.

When we don't know how to process anger in a healthy way, things can go wrong. If we suppress it, it builds. And if we lash out, we might say or do things we regret. That's why we need safe, intentional ways to release that energy. Pillow screaming is one of those ways.

Here's how to do it:

1. **Grab a pillow** and hold it firmly with both hands.
2. **Bring the pillow to your face**, not to suffocate yourself, but to muffle the sound.
3. Then... **scream**.

You can let your whole body move as you scream: stomp your feet, shake your arms, or jump up and down. Let the energy move through you. Let it out fully and without holding back.

This is a safe, effective method for releasing anger, stress, or frustration. You can do it standing, sitting, or even kneeling on the floor or on a bed. Make it your own.

And the next time anger rises and you feel it building in your body, remember: you have this tool. You don't need to suppress your emotions or let them explode, you can express them safely and fully. You might not be able to apply this technique right away. In that case, I suggest you take a few deep breaths, name your emotions and commit to doing this technique later that day.

As part of your daily routine, I invite you to try this technique today. Reflect on a current or past situation that incites anger or frustration, and use the Pillow Screaming technique to process that emotion. Remember, whenever you need to deal with anger or frustration, this method is both simple and effective.

Daily Routine 14

1. Do the Heart to Yes technique.
2. Practice mindfulness meditation for ten minutes.
3. Journal for five to ten minutes.
4. Practice the Pillow Screaming technique.
    - Find a safe space where you are alone, and won't be distracted or interrupted.
    - Take a pillow and hold it firmly with both hands on each side.
    - Bury your face into the pillow.
    - As you scream, listen to your body and allow it to move naturally; you can stomp your feet, shake your arms, do whatever feels right; respect your body.
    - Remember to be gentle with yourself, be compassionate. It might take multiple sessions to process certain emotions, be patient with yourself.

If you'd like to take that release a step further, Pillow Beating builds on the same principle: a safe and physical expression of strong emotions.

Pillow Beating

Before we move on to the next technique, there's something important to keep in mind: all of the somatic tools you're learning in this chapter can be used for as little or as long as you need. Some days you might want to work through an emotion in one deep session. Other days, you may only need a few moments or choose to return to it across multiple days. Let yourself be flexible. Let the emotions guide you.

Now, let's talk about another highly effective technique for processing anger and frustration: Pillow Beating.

This method is especially powerful when you're dealing with intense emotional energy whether from a current situation or one from your past. And yes, as the name implies, you will need a pillow.

Why a pillow? Because it's safe. Hitting a wall, a piece of furniture, or worse, another person, isn't a healthy or constructive option. The pillow provides a soft, forgiving surface that allows your body to fully express itself without risk of harm.

Here's how to do it:

1. Place a pillow on your bed.
2. Stand in front of it, or kneel on the bed if that feels more stable for you.
3. Raise both arms overhead, as if holding a bat. Stretch your torso, especially your abdominal wall, as you prepare to move.
4. Then, in one swift motion, bring your arms down and strike the pillow.
5. If it feels natural, add a scream or vocal release as you do it. For example, you can let out a moaning sound.

Repeat this motion several times, letting your body release whatever needs to come up and out. You might find yourself wanting to shout, cry, or laugh, that's all part of the process. Let it move through you. Allow yourself the freedom to express your emotions fully.

I often use this technique when I notice anger bubbling beneath the surface whether from something fresh or something I've carried for years. It helps me explore those deeper layers of emotion and release them from my body. Every time I do it, I feel more grounded and at peace afterward, almost like the storm inside has passed and left behind a quiet calm.

One note: this technique can be physically intense. It may draw on more energy than you expect. So make sure to give yourself time to rest afterward. Be gentle with yourself. Listen to what your body needs.

This practice has become one of my favorites because of how effective it is at restoring emotional balance. It may look simple, but its impact is profound.

As part of your daily routine, I invite you to try this today. Think of something that's stirred anger or frustration in you whether recent or from a long time ago, and use the Pillow Beating technique as a way to release it safely.

Let this be another tool in your journey of emotional resilience and self-liberation.

Daily Routine 15

1. Do the Heart to Yes technique.
2. Practice mindfulness meditation for ten minutes.
3. Journal for five to ten minutes.
4. Practice the Pillow Beating technique for five minutes.
    - Positioning: You can either go on your knees on your bed or, if your bed is high enough, stand beside it and place the pillow in front of you.
    - Hand Placement: Put your hands as if you were holding a bat over your head. Stretch your abdominal wall.

- Striking: Strike the pillow hard in one motion. You can also add a scream as you strike.

While Pillow Beating helps us release emotions in a burst of energy, sometimes what we need is the opposite: a full-body reset. That's where Tensing and Releasing comes in.

Tensing and Releasing

Sometimes the emotions we carry aren't explosive like anger, they're subtle, like stress or tension that quietly weighs us down. And in these situations, Tensing and Releasing is helpful. This technique is one of the simplest and most effective ways to reduce stress and calm the nervous system.

It's exactly what it sounds like. You tense your entire body, hold that tension for a few seconds, and then release everything all at once. This powerful somatic technique helps move stress out of the body and creates a deep sense of relaxation in its place.

Personally, this technique has been a game changer for me. As someone living with cerebral palsy, I experience frequent muscle spasms, and Tensing and Releasing has helped calm my body and soothe my muscles. It's a way to give our whole system a reset.

You can do this practice lying down, sitting, or even standing, though lying down is often the most comfortable. Here's how it works:

1. Begin by tensing every muscle in your body. Tighten your fists, your arms, your legs, your toes, your shoulders and even your butt cheeks.
2. Hold that tension as long as you comfortably can. Feel your whole body engaging with effort.
3. When you're ready, release all the tension at once. Let it go completely, soften every part of you.
4. Pause. Notice how you feel.
5. Repeat the process as many times as you like.

You may be surprised at how calming this simple action can be. After just one round, I often feel a wave of relaxation moving through my body. It's like my muscles are saying: "Thank you for letting go."

Now, I'd like to offer an optional enhancement to this practice, one that draws in the power of imagination and amplifies the emotional release: visualization.

As you prepare to tense your body, imagine the stress you're carrying as an image. Maybe it's a dark ball lodged in your back, a heavy block in your chest, or a spiky mass hovering around you. Give it a color, a texture, a weight.

Hold that image in your mind as you tighten your muscles.

Then, as you release, imagine that shape transforming, changing color, shifting form, shrinking, floating away, or disappearing completely. You might see it dissolve into light, or float off like a balloon. Visualize whatever brings you the most relief and freedom.

And here's something important: after a few rounds, once that image has changed into something that feels freeing or light, you don't need to go back to the original form. Let the new image remain, even if you continue with the tensing and releasing. You're retraining your nervous system to associate release with freedom, not just the absence of tension.

The imagery is personal. What feels freeing for you may be different than what works for me. Trust your intuition. This is your practice.

As part of your daily rhythm, I invite you to try this technique. Set aside five to ten minutes.

Tense. Release. Visualize. Repeat.

Then, simply notice the calm that follows.

Above all, be gentle with yourself. Let this practice be a gift of relief, something you can return to whenever you need to let go and find ease again.

Daily Routine 16

1. Do the Heart to Yes technique.
2. Practice mindfulness meditation for ten minutes.
3. Journal for five to ten minutes.
4. Practice the Tensing and Releasing technique. Tense every part of your body as tightly as you can, whether you're sitting or lying down, and then release completely. You can add the visualization described above to enhance the stress relief benefits. Do this for five to ten minutes.

When life throws us curveballs, difficult feelings come in and we can quickly conclude that life is unfair. And Chest Beating is especially effective when despair takes a hold of us.

Chest Beating

It's completely normal to feel despair and sadness when things don't turn out the way we imagined or the way we hoped they would. What's not helpful is getting stuck in those emotions. But repressing them isn't helpful either. So what are we supposed to do?

Mindfulness and journaling can help us become aware of these feelings and begin to move through them. But sometimes, the emotions are too big for words. That's where Chest Beating is most helpful.

The Chest Beating technique is a simple but powerful way to physically process deep emotions like sadness, despair, and frustration. It's especially helpful when we're wrestling with a sense of injustice, when something just feels unfair and we don't know what to do with it.

Here's how it works. Extend your arms outward and begin gently beating your chest. You can use one hand or both, alternating sides or moving in rhythm, like King Kong claiming his place on the skyscraper. Add a vocalization if it feels natural. You might want to repeat "ah," or another sound that expresses what you're feeling. You can even stomp your feet like a child having a tantrum. **This isn't about performance, it's about permission. Giving yourself permission to feel.**

For me, this technique is a way of accepting not just the situation, but my emotional response to it. Sometimes life truly isn't fair. Chest Beating gives me a way to honor that truth and release the emotional charge it carries. It drains the overwhelming energy of despair and allows me to feel sadness fully, without being consumed by it.

The result? I feel calmer. More centered. More grounded. I'm better able to see clearly and respond with balance, rather than swinging between extremes. It's one of the techniques that consistently helps me return to myself.

As part of your daily routine today, I invite you to try this. Think of a situation, either from your past or your present, that makes you feel hopeless, stuck, or sad. Let that feeling rise. Then use the Chest Beating technique to process it. Move the energy, give your body permission to express, and allow the emotion to flow through.

This is how we reclaim our power, not by denying our feelings, but by moving through them fully.

Daily Routine 17

1. Do the Heart to Yes technique.
2. Practice mindfulness meditation for ten minutes.
3. Journal for five to ten minutes.
4. Practice the Chest Beating technique. Extend your arms outward and begin gently beating your chest, alternating sides and consider using your voice to express your feeling through sound.

Just as Chest Beating helps us process despair and frustration, Arching Your Back works in a similar way and opens the body to release grief and sadness.

Arching Your Back

Arching Your Back is a powerful somatic technique for releasing deep emotional tension, especially feelings of sadness, despair, hopelessness, loneliness, and abandonment.

This practice is simple but profound. It works by physically opening up the chest and lungs, areas that often close in or collapse when we're feeling overwhelmed or discouraged. By intentionally reversing that posture, we create space for emotional release and healing.

Here's how to do it:

1. **Stand tall** with your feet rooted firmly on the ground.
2. **Extend your arms** out to your sides in a T-shape.
3. **Gently arch your back,** lifting your chest and opening your heart. You don't need to bend deeply, just enough to feel the stretch across the front of your body.
4. **Let your head tip back** slightly if it feels comfortable.
5. **Make a sound.** Let out a sigh, a groan, a breathy "ahhh," or any other vocalization that your body naturally wants to release.
6. **Stomp your feet,** if it helps move the energy more fully through your system.
7. **Repeat as needed.** Do the movement and sound as many times as feels helpful. Let your body guide you.

When I do this technique, I often imagine I'm saying, "Take it all. I need help." For me, it's a moment of surrender, a release of control and a call for support. It's as if I'm physically opening myself to receive whatever healing or relief is available.

This technique has been especially powerful for me after my separation. It helped me process not just that recent grief, but older wounds too, feelings of abandonment, loneliness, or not belonging that surfaced from childhood. Sometimes I remembered moments where I felt like I wasn't like everyone else... like I didn't quite fit in or wasn't wanted. And while those feelings may not have reflected reality, they were real to me. Arching my back gave me a way to feel those emotions and let them move through.

As part of your daily routine today, I invite you to try this technique. Recall a time, either recent or distant, when you felt sadness, loneliness, or abandonment. Let that memory come up gently. Then practice arching your back and allow your body to express what it needs to. You can do it just once or several times. Even a little bit can go a long way.

And remember: the more you practice these tools, the more naturally they'll come to you when you need them. Whether it's mindfulness, journaling, or a somatic technique like this one, you're building a toolkit you can return to again and again.

Let yourself feel. Let your body speak. Let the energy move.

Daily Routine 18

1. Do the Heart to Yes technique.
2. Practice mindfulness meditation for ten minutes.
3. Journal for five to ten minutes.
4. Practice the Arching Your Back technique.
    - Stand tall and ground your feet.
    - Extend your arms out to your sides in a T-shape.
    - Gently arch your back.
    - Let your head tip back slightly.

- Make a sound of release.
- Stomp your feet (optional).
- Repeat as needed. Let yourself go there! Dare to take enough time to become vulnerable and raw. Give yourself the permission to cry.

Punching and Kicking

Now let's look at another practice for releasing anger, one that directly helps us connect to our boundaries: Punching and Kicking. Some say that anger and frustration often arise when a boundary has been crossed, either by someone else or by ourselves. I find this model helpful because it gives us a clear framework to work with. It invites us to ask: What boundary was crossed? What boundary didn't I uphold?

This Punching and Kicking somatic technique is one of the most effective ways I know to process that kind of emotional energy. It's not about being violent. It's not about harming anyone. It's about reclaiming our power and moving the charge of anger and frustration through our body rather than letting it stay trapped inside.

There's one important distinction in how we do this: we use open palms, not clenched fists. For me, the open palm is symbolic. It says "Stop". It says "No more." It helps me reclaim my voice and my boundaries in a healthy way.

Here's how to do it:

1. **Find a safe, private space** where you have room to move your arms and legs freely without risk of hurting yourself or others.

2. **Stand with your feet flat on the floor, in a stable stance.** Feel rooted and grounded.
3. **Begin to punch forward using your open palms.** Let your arms swing powerfully, one at a time or both together.
4. **As you punch, say "No!"** out loud with force and intention. You can repeat it over and over, letting the emotion rise and move.
5. **Add kicking if it feels natural.** You can stomp your feet or throw short kicks, whatever helps move the energy through your body.
6. **Keep going** for a few minutes, or as long as you feel the need. Let your body and breath guide you.

This practice has been profoundly liberating for me. It has helped me release pent-up anger and also reflect on the boundaries I once struggled and sometimes failed to set in the past, especially in close relationships. For a long time, I thought of myself simply as a very patient person and in some ways, I was. *But I also lacked the skills to assert my boundaries clearly, and that created confusion and frustration for both me and my loved ones.*

Through this technique, I started to see where I had compromised too much. Where I had silenced myself instead of saying no. And that awareness helped me grow.

So while this method is great for releasing anger, it also invites reflection. Where do we need stronger boundaries? **Where have we been saying yes when we wanted to say no?**

As part of your daily routine today, I invite you to try this technique. Set aside about five minutes. Find a safe space, tune into a moment, past or present, when your boundaries were crossed, and use this practice to explore and release the emotion.

Let your body say what words couldn't. Let your energy move. Let your "No" be heard.

Daily Routine 19

1. Do the Heart to Yes technique.
2. Practice mindfulness meditation for ten minutes.
3. Journal for five to ten minutes.
4. Practice the Punching and Kicking technique.
   - Find a safe, private space
   - Stand with your feet flat on the floor, in a stable stance.
   - Begin to punch forward using your open palms.
   - As you punch, say "No!"
   - Add kicking if it feels natural.
   - Keep going as long as you feel the need.

The next somatic technique, Dancing and Shaking, is also very energetic and great at processing intense emotions.

Dancing and Shaking

There was a time when I went to an ecstatic dance feeling incredibly low. I was deeply depressed that day, my spirit barely hanging on. I had already been attending ecstatic dances for a while, so I was in good shape physically. But emotionally, I was in a dark place.

Before we continue, I want to offer a gentle content note here: this story briefly touches on suicidal thoughts. If you're not in a place to read that right now, please feel free to skip ahead to the Daily Routine section. Your well-being matters most.

That night, my intention was grim. I told myself: "I'm going to dance to drain all this pain or die trying." That was how empty and desperate I felt. So I moved. I danced as hard as I could. I shook. I stomped. I let my whole body speak the grief I couldn't put into words. And at the end of it, something cracked open. I dropped to the floor and said to the universe: "That's it. I can't take this anymore. I need something good to happen."

It was raw. But it was real. And for the first time in what felt like forever, I had a sliver of faith again. *Something about giving myself fully to the dance helped me let go of all the ways I was trying to force life to look a certain way.* And in that surrender, I found a tiny bit of freedom. That night showed me something profound: dance can be more than movement. It can be healing. And that's why dancing and shaking is such a powerful tool.

Dancing can do that. It's a physical prayer, a way of expressing emotions and making space for vulnerability. When we dance—really dance—we stop trying to look good. We stop performing. We move the way our body wants to move. We allow feelings and thoughts to rise and fall like waves.

Sometimes, when I dance, I notice things that surprise me, like how quickly I can still feel jealousy, or how easily I get caught in comparison. But instead of judging those feelings, I accept them and I keep moving. I let the dance process them for me.

And you don't need a group or a special event to do this. You can dance and shake on your own, in your bedroom, your kitchen, your living room, wherever you feel free.

Here's how to do it:

1. **Choose music that matches your emotional state.** If you're feeling sad, pick something soulful or heartfelt. If you want to lift your energy, choose something upbeat or empowering.
2. **Press play and start moving.** Let your body respond to the rhythm. There are no wrong moves. You don't need to follow steps, just follow your instinct.
3. **Allow yourself to express.** You might cry. You might sigh. You might growl or laugh. Give your body permission to do what it needs.
4. **Add shaking if it feels natural.** Shaking can be done as part of the dance or on its own. Let your arms, legs, and torso shake loosely. This is a powerful way to move stuck energy.
5. **Dance for at least a few songs.** Two, three, or four songs is a great start. Let your body decide when it's had enough.
6. **When you're done, pause and feel.** Notice how your body feels. What shifted? What was released?

You might be surprised by how healing this can be. Shaking, in particular, is a natural stress reliever, used by animals and humans alike to discharge excess energy from the nervous system. It can calm you down, help you cry, or even give you energy when you're feeling low. We'll explore that energizing side later in this chapter.

For today, I invite you to try this practice as part of your daily routine. Choose a few songs. Close the door. And let go. Whether it looks like salsa, chaotic shaking, or barely moving at all—it doesn't matter. What matters is that it's real.

This is your time. Your space. Your dance.

Daily Routine 20

1. Do the Heart to Yes technique.
2. Practice mindfulness meditation for ten minutes.
3. Journal for five to ten minutes.
4. Practice dancing for the length of two to five songs and practice shaking.
   - Choose music that matches your emotional state.
   - Press play and start moving.
   - Allow yourself to express.
   - Add shaking. Consider practicing shaking on its own, especially when you need to release emotions quickly. It's an effective and efficient way to break away from an unresourceful state.
   - Dance for at least a few songs.
   - When you're done, pause and feel.

After a high-energy practice like Dancing and Shaking, it's helpful to remember that somatic work can also be subtle. Sometimes, simply noticing and naming sensations is enough.

Speaking Sensations

Not every somatic practice requires big movement or sound. Sometimes, simply noticing and speaking sensations is just what we need. It is a powerful technique that helps us regulate our emotions by naming what we feel in our body, without judgment, and without the need to explain why.

In a way, this practice builds on something we explored earlier in this book: naming your emotions. But here, we go even more basic. Instead of labeling emotions, we simply notice and speak the physical sensations present in our body. That's it. No stories. No explanations. Just sensation.

You can do this practice seated, lying down, or even standing. Start by getting still.

1. Close your eyes and take a few deep breaths.
2. Bring your awareness behind your eyes. Feel that space.
3. Gently shift your attention to the center of your head, between your ears.
4. Breathe naturally for a few moments. Let yourself settle.
5. When you feel ready, begin to move your awareness slowly through your body.

The goal isn't to scan every inch. Instead, just notice where your attention is drawn. Ask: "What physical sensations are present right now?" You might notice things like:

- I feel a pulsing in my right shoulder.
- There's tightness in my jaw.
- My left hand feels warm.
- There's a heavy feeling in my chest.
- I feel numb on the left side of my head.

Name the sensations exactly as you experience them. Not why they're there. Not what they mean. Just the physical experience.

If you catch yourself attaching a story or an emotion to the sensation like "I feel tight because I'm stressed at work," gently let that go. Come back to the physical layer: tightness in the chest, heat in the face, buzzing in the legs.

Bring an attitude of compassion and non-judgment. **We're simply witnessing what is**.

You can also practice this with someone else, especially when emotions are high. Instead of saying, I'm angry, you might say, I notice tightness in my throat and pressure in my chest. That level of awareness can create space for honest connection, rather than defensiveness or reactivity.

Here's the thing: we can argue with emotions. We can debate whether we should feel angry, or sad, or hurt. But we can't argue with sensation. Sensation just is. And by focusing on the physical, we can gently detach from emotional intensity and come back to center, giving each other the space we need to be curious, instead of defensive, and the time to understand one another.

As part of your daily routine today, I invite you to try this practice. Find a quiet moment. Sit or lie down. Close your eyes. Move inward. And simply name what you feel in your body.

Tightness in my shoulders. Buzzing in my legs. Warmth in my belly. Numbness behind my eyes.

Just that. And see what shifts.

Daily Routine 21

1. Do the Heart to Yes technique.
2. Practice mindfulness meditation for ten minutes.
3. Journal for five to ten minutes.
4. Practice the Speaking Sensations technique.

- Gently shift your attention to the center of your head, between your ears.
- Breathe naturally for a few moments.
- Begin to move your awareness slowly through your body, noticing physical sensations without justification and storytelling.

Getting Motivated

So far, the techniques we've explored focus on releasing heavy emotions. But somatic practices can also generate light and uplifting emotions: they can boost motivation and confidence.

The way we hold our body, our posture, our breath, our movement, has a huge impact on how we feel. Somatic techniques aren't just for releasing emotions like sadness or anger. They're also powerful tools for building energy, confidence, and clarity.

Let me show you what I mean. Try this with me:

1. Lower your head and roll your shoulders forward. Let your breath become shallow and your chest collapse a little. Maybe even sigh or groan quietly as if you're sad or defeated.
2. Stay like that for a few seconds and notice how it makes you feel.

Chances are, you feel a dip in energy. Maybe even less confident. That's not your imagination. Our posture affects our nervous system, our hormones, and our mood. Now, shake it off by literally shaking your body.

Now let's try the opposite:

1. Stand or sit tall. Roll your shoulders back. Lift your chin slightly. Take a few deep, intentional breaths.
2. Breathe like you matter. Like your presence makes a difference (because it does).

Can you feel the shift? More alert, more open, more powerful.

It's not magic. It's your body telling your brain: I'm safe. I'm strong. I'm ready.

Of course, this isn't a cure-all. If you're exhausted and sleep deprived, you must get rest. If you're hungry, eat nourishing food. These are non-negotiable. Honoring your body is not a sign of weakness or a waste of time. It's an essential building block for becoming unstoppable.

Power Posing

One of the quickest ways to tap into motivation is through posture. Power Posing is a practice I return to often when I need a fast confidence boost before a meeting, a conversation, or a challenge.

You can also use movement to supercharge this shift. I often combine these posture and breath adjustments with music and energizing gestures. Here are a few of my go-to moves:

- Stretching tall and wide, opening the chest and arms.
- Shaking out the arms and legs with a burst of energy.

- Deep, powerful breaths: in through the nose, out through the mouth.
- Air punches! Fist-pumping like Rocky Balboa. Yes, it looks a little silly but it works.
- Placing a hand on your heart and saying, "Yes," like you mean it.
- Jumping up and down.

The goal isn't to follow a routine perfectly, it's to feel alive. Find movements that you enjoy. Better yet, associate them with a memory when you felt unstoppable. That anchoring makes the effect even stronger.

You don't need to wait for the right mood to begin. Sometimes, movement creates the mood.

As part of your daily routine today, try this out. Put on music you love. Move your body. Find a gesture or rhythm that makes you feel alive, inspired, and powerful. Breathe like someone who knows their worth.

You already have what you need. It's just waiting to be activated. Together, these practices show the wide range of somatic tools, from calming the nervous system to energizing your body and mind. As we wrap up this chapter, here's how to keep them integrated in your daily life.

Daily Routine 22

1. Do the Heart to Yes technique.
2. Practice mindfulness meditation for ten minutes.
3. Journal for five to ten minutes.
4. Use Power Posing to get motivated!
   - Shaking
   - Jumping

- Stretching
- Air punching
- Hand on heart and say yes!
- Come up with your own motivational move :-)

Practice as Needed

Throughout this chapter, I've invited you to explore somatic techniques daily. These practices, whether it's shaking, screaming, arching, or dancing, help move emotion through the body and restore balance to the nervous system. They're powerful tools, and I hope you've started to feel that power for yourself.

From this point on, your daily routine won't include somatic techniques every single day. I'll continue to suggest specific somatic techniques in later chapters where they apply, so you can deepen your learning and integration.

But I want to leave you with this: when a strong emotion comes up, sadness, frustration, fear, grief, reach for what you've learned here, and practice a somatic technique.

Yes, mindfulness and journaling are incredibly effective tools. They'll continue to serve you well. And at the same time, somatic techniques give you a different kind of access: they let your body take the lead.

Your body holds emotion. It stores memories. And it knows how to heal, if you give it the chance to move, breathe, and release.

So don't wait for the perfect moment. Let somatic work become part of how you care for yourself. When you feel stuck, anxious, heavy, or even overwhelmed with joy: move! Use your breath. Use your voice. Let your body speak.

Because the more you explore yourself with these techniques, the more you'll understand yourself. And the more emotional energy you release, the freer, lighter, and more grounded you become.

Keep going.

Keep practicing.

Let your body show you the way.

In the next chapter, we'll return to the power of the mind as we explore self-hypnosis.

7. Self-Hypnosis

I first learned hypnosis from Mike Mandel, an incredible hypnotist based in Toronto, Canada. With over fifty years of experience, Mike is one of the best in the field, and I feel lucky to have trained with him.

In this chapter, we're going to explore self-hypnosis. I'll guide you through everything you need to know to get started and start using it, not only as a tool for relaxation, but as a way to create meaningful, lasting change in your life.

A Brief History of Hypnosis

The story of hypnosis is anything but ordinary. It's a winding journey full of curious characters, questionable theories, and groundbreaking discoveries. Over the centuries, hypnosis has evolved from mystical showmanship into a respected therapeutic practice and the truth is, the real history is even more fascinating than the myths.

The Mesmerizing Beginning

Our tale starts in the late 1700s with Franz Anton Mesmer, an eccentric figure who believed that an invisible force, called animal magnetism, flowed through all living things. Mesmer claimed he could manipulate this force to heal illness. His treatments involved patients sitting around a large wooden tub called a baquet, holding metal rods supposedly charged with magnetic energy, while Mesmer himself, dressed in a robe and turban, moved about the room with a wand, accompanied by the eerie sounds of a glass harmonica.

Patients would twitch, tremble, sometimes collapse, and occasionally… get better. Mesmer even "magnetized" trees, inviting people to touch them for healing. Sometimes it worked, though the same results happened when people touched the wrong tree, suggesting belief and expectation, rather than any actual magnetic current, was the true healing force.

Despite being eventually discredited, Mesmer's methods were far less dangerous than the medical practices of his day (like bloodletting), and his emphasis on expectation laid the groundwork for the hypnotic techniques that followed. While Mesmer's theories faded, his emphasis on expectation paved the way for pioneers who applied hypnosis to medicine in practical and sometimes life-saving ways.

The Surgical Pioneers

In the 1800s, Scottish surgeon James Esdaile brought mesmerism to India, where he performed hundreds of operations, including major surgeries, without chemical anesthesia, using hypnotic states to block pain. The so-called Esdaile state took hours to induce, but it reduced shock and infection and survival rates improved.

Around the same time in England, physician John Elliotson championed mesmerism until his career collapsed after he publicly supported two fraudulent psychic sisters.

From Mysticism to Science

The real scientific turn came with James Braid, a Manchester-based surgeon who witnessed a mesmerist's show and decided to investigate. Braid discovered that hypnosis had nothing to do with magnetic forces, *it was the result of focused attention and suggestion.* He developed techniques involving eye fixation and intense concentration, and introduced the idea that a single, absorbing thought could lead to trance.

Braid didn't invent the word hypnosis, he called it hypnotism. Hypnosis was coined in France after his death. Braid's work stripped away much of the mystical baggage, making hypnosis more acceptable to the medical community.

Freud and the Birth of Psychoanalysis

Sigmund Freud experimented with hypnosis in the late 1800s, using it to explore the unconscious mind. He was influenced by the work of Charcot and Bernheim who were prominent figures in late 19th-century neurology, psychiatry and hypnosis. However, he never became skilled at inducing trance and eventually abandoned it in favor of free association which led to the birth of psychoanalysis. Ironically, while Freud stepped away from hypnosis, his work kept alive the central idea that the unconscious mind plays a vital role in shaping thoughts and behavior.

Milton Erickson and the Modern Era

Fast forward to the 20th century, and we meet Milton H. Erickson, often regarded as the most influential hypnotist in history. Stricken with polio as a teenager, Erickson learned to observe people's behavior in extraordinary detail and developed ways to communicate directly with the unconscious through storytelling, metaphor, and indirect suggestion.

His approach was gentle, conversational, and deeply respectful of the individual. Rather than giving orders, Erickson created opportunities for people to discover their own solutions. His influence extended beyond hypnosis into fields like psychotherapy, coaching, and even modern NLP (Neuro-Linguistic Programming).

Become Part of the Legacy

From Mesmer's magnetic wands to Erickson's subtle metaphors, hypnosis has traveled a long road. Along the way, it's moved from a mysterious spectacle to a well-respected tool for personal change, pain control, and emotional healing. In 1955 the British Medical Association endorsed hypnosis as a valuable medical tool, and in 1958 the American Medical Association formally recognized it as a viable therapeutic technique. Today, we know hypnosis is not magic, it's a learnable skill that uses focus, imagination, and suggestion to engage the most powerful parts of the mind.

When you practice self-hypnosis, you're tapping into a tradition that has been evolving for over 250 years, a tradition shaped by both the visionaries and the skeptics. And now, you get to add your own story to that history. Which brings us to the most practical question: what, exactly, is hypnosis and how do we use it?

What is Hypnosis?

Let's start with a simple but important idea: hypnosis is both a state and a process. It's a state of focused attention and relaxed awareness that makes a person more open to suggestions. Hypnosis is also a specific process we apply and maintain and I'll walk you through that step by step.

Why would we want to get into a hypnotic trance in the first place? Why practice hypnosis or self-hypnosis at all?

The answer is simple but profound: **because our minds are incredibly powerful.**

To understand how hypnosis works, it helps to think of the mind as having two parts: the conscious mind and the unconscious (or subconscious) mind.

Your conscious mind is everything you're aware of at the moment. For example, if I ask you what your phone number is, you'll recall it, that's your conscious mind at work. But before I asked, you weren't actively thinking about your phone number. So where was that information? It was in your unconscious mind.

The unconscious mind stores all of our memories and life experiences. It also regulates the automatic functions of the body, such as digestion, heart rate, and breathing. Breathing is a bit unique, because while it's mostly unconscious, we can choose to control it consciously. But many other bodily functions are completely regulated by the unconscious. The unconscious mind is a powerful, hidden engine beneath our conscious awareness, quietly guiding much of our thinking, behavior, and decisions.

When we enter a trance state through hypnosis, we gain direct access to the unconscious mind by bypassing the critical faculty.

The critical faculty is the part of the conscious mind that analyzes, judges, and filters information, preventing automatic acceptance of suggestions that conflict with existing beliefs. We can think of it as a bouncer at the door of a nightclub, only letting in people with a specific look. It only lets in ideas, patterns, and beliefs that fit what's already programmed into our minds. This is why we need to bypass it to change old patterns and introduce new ways of seeing and experiencing life.

By entering hypnosis and deepening the trance, we can create powerful shifts: changing the way we relate to our past, influencing how we see the future, and rapidly forming new habits, behavior and beliefs.

Thanks to the brain's natural capacity for change, what neuroscience calls neuroplasticity, hypnosis becomes a direct pathway for transformation. When we bypass the conscious mind and work with the unconscious, we literally create new neural pathways. Our brain physically changes. These changes can be deep and long-lasting. In some cases, just one hypnosis session can have a permanent impact. Other times, it might take a few repetitions or occasional reinforcement but the shifts are still significant.

In this chapter, you'll learn how to:

- Put yourself into a trance safely, effectively and efficiently
- Access inner resources for healing, growth, and clarity
- Shift your perspective on the past and future and
- Change the way you relate to yourself.

Self-hypnosis is one of the most efficient and empowering tools you can learn to change your life. Let's get you started.

Now that you know more about hypnosis, I'll give you step-by-step instructions to guide yourself into your first trance so you can begin working with your unconscious mind and unlock the power that's already within you.

Self-Hypnosis

When we practice self-hypnosis, we are both the subject and the hypnotist. In this chapter, I will show you two ways of working on yourself while in a hypnotic trance.

In the first variation, we go into hypnosis, let the unconscious do all the work, and then come out of the trance. In the second variation, we go into trance and then, as the hypnotist, direct the work using one of the techniques you'll discover in this chapter. We will explore two specific techniques: the Timeline and the Ego State.

To practice self-hypnosis, we follow four simple steps: **pre-hypnosis**, **induction**, **work**, and **coming out of trance**. Let's explore each step together.

The Pre-Hypnosis Step

In the pre-hypnosis step, we make a contract with ourselves. We tell ourselves how long we want to go into hypnosis, specify the work we want to accomplish, and decide how we want to feel after we come out of trance. This usually falls into two outcomes: either we want to be refreshed, energized, and ready for the day or we want to feel sleepy, ready to drift into a deep rest and transition into sleep.

Key Steps:

- Decide how long you will remain in hypnosis.
- Choose the work or intention for the session.
- Decide how you want to feel afterward: energized or ready for sleep.

The Hypnosis Induction

After making this personal contract, we do the hypnosis induction. A hypnosis induction is a process or set of techniques used to guide someone into a hypnotic state, where their attention is highly focused, their mind is more open to suggestion, and they can access deeper levels of relaxation and concentration. The first one I teach you is a simple but powerful induction, taught to me by my mentor Mike Mandel. He calls it *Breathing With the Eyes*. I find it to be one of the easiest ways to induce a hypnotic trance.

Breathing With the Eyes

We start by sitting or lying down. If you tend to fall asleep quickly, sitting is better, so you enter trance rather than slipping directly into sleep. Next, we choose a fixed point located across the room and above our natural eye level, and pretend to breathe with our eyes.

As we inhale deeply, we open our eyes wide, as if air could flow in through them. As we exhale, we let our eyes gently close, imagining our eyelids becoming heavy. It may feel a little silly, but it is surprisingly powerful. After doing this three to five times, we simply keep our eyes closed and allow ourselves to drop inward. If it takes a bit longer, keep "breathing with your eyes" until it feels more comfortable to keep your eyes shut. With practice, it will get easier and quicker. When closing our eyes, we can also slightly tilt our chin toward our chest. And the moment our eyelids feel like they want to stay close, we let them.

Of course, never do this while driving or doing anything that requires your full attention.

Key Steps

- Sit or lie down (choose sitting if you tend to fall asleep).
- Fix your gaze on a point across the room. Choose a point slightly above your natural eye level, so your gaze angles upward.
- Inhale deeply while opening your eyes wide ("breathing through your eyes"). **Exaggerate the movement as if you were taking big breaths with your eyes, stretching your eyelids upward.**
- Exhale slowly while closing your eyes, **feeling your eyelids grow heavy.**
- Repeat three to five times or until it feels more comfortable to keep your eyes closed, then keep them closed. It may take longer at first; with practice it becomes easier and quicker.

Progressive Relaxation

Progressive relaxation can feel slow when doing hypnosis with another person, but for self-hypnosis it's a highly effective induction. Relaxation naturally reduces stress, and deep breathing alone can help us slip into trance. If you already have a favorite relaxation technique, feel free to use it to go into hypnosis before moving into a deepening method. The goal is simply to progressively relax both body and mind.

One way to do this is by using the Body Scan technique we explored in the last chapter, but instead of focussing on noticing, we focus on relaxing the body. Visit each part of your body, and with every exhale, silently say to yourself, "more relaxed." Another approach is to imagine gentle waves of water rising up over the body, first the feet, then the legs, then the abdomen and chest, and finally the neck and head. As each wave passes, the area feels heavier, calmer, and more at ease.

Once your whole body and mind are softened, you can move deeper into trance using the staircase method described in the next section.

Key Steps

- Sit or lie down in a comfortable position.
- Choose a relaxation approach: body scan or rising waves of water.
- With each exhale, release tension and quietly say, "more relaxed."
- Allow each area of the body to grow heavier and calmer.
- Once fully relaxed, move on to the staircase method to deepen trance.

Visualization as Induction

Visualization is powerful because the brain often responds to a vivid imagined experience as though it were real. This makes visualization not only a tool for transformation, but also an effective way to enter hypnosis. Many people think they *can't visualize* because they expect movie-like images in their mind but that's rarely the case. Everyone does it differently. The images come in different shapes, forms, impressions and even feelings. If you struggle to visualize, pretend you can for now, and with practice it will become easier.

One way to use visualization as an induction is to imagine a soothing mist of color surrounding you, perhaps pale blue, soft green, or any shade that feels calming to you. With each breath, inhale the mist and allow it to relax you more deeply. As the mist fills your body and mind, you become calmer, heavier, and more at ease. Once you feel fully relaxed, you can move on to a deepening technique to enter trance more deeply.

Another powerful variation was introduced by Milton H. Erickson. He invited his patients to imagine a metronome, keeping their attention on its steady, rhythmic swing. Simply attending to the metronome's steady swing draws you inward and allows trance to emerge naturally.

Key Steps

- Close your eyes and imagine a calming color mist surrounding you.
- With each inhale, breathe in the soothing mist.
- Allow the mist to fill your body, relaxing you completely.
- Alternatively, imagine a metronome and watch its steady rhythm.
- Once relaxed, move into a deepening technique to enter trance fully.

Eye Fixation

In the Breathing With the Eyes method we already touched on the idea of eye fixation, but it's worth exploring on its own. This method goes back to James Braid, who discovered that by fixating on an object or light, people naturally slip into trance. It's a very quick and effective induction.

To practice, sit comfortably and choose a fixed point across the room. Make sure the point is slightly above your natural line of sight so that your eyes are angled upward. As you stare **intently** at this spot, imagine your eyes becoming more and more tired. Simply pretending they are heavy is often enough. Soon, they will want to close on their own. When they do, allow them to close, and let yourself drift into trance.

Key Steps

- Sit comfortably and select a point across the room.
- Ensure the point is slightly above your natural eye level.
- Fix your gaze steadily on this spot.
- Pretend your eyes are growing tired and heavy.
- When your eyelids close, allow yourself to drift into trance.

Just Go Into Trance

After you've experienced hypnosis a few times, your unconscious mind begins to recognize the process and can return there more easily. At that point, you can simply decide to go into trance. Milton H. Erickson often told his patients to "just go into hypnosis," and they did. With practice, you'll find that suggestion alone can be enough.

To make this even more effective, you can use imagery like a dimmer switch or an on/off switch. In the Visualization++ chapter, we'll explore this further, but you can already apply it here. Imagine turning the switch down or off, and with it, letting yourself drop inward into trance.

Key Steps

- Close your eyes and breathe deeply.
- Tell yourself to "just go into trance."
- Allow your unconscious to guide you into the familiar state.
- For support, imagine a dimmer switch or on/off switch being turned down.
- As the switch lowers, feel yourself slipping quickly into trance.

Deepening the Trance

Once we complete the hypnosis induction, we keep our eyes closed and deepen the trance to get to a place where it's easier to do the work. Going into hypnosis already allows us to bypass the critical faculty. But deepening the trance takes us further into a place of greater comfort, serenity, and focus. Going deeper into trance helps us maintain the hypnosis state and process, and do excellent transformational work.

One way to deepen the trance is to imagine a staircase leading down. We go down step by step, pretending we are sinking deeper into our unconscious. Personally, I like to imagine it getting darker and quieter as I descend. I recommend going down ten steps at first. If you wish, you can add another level of ten steps, but beyond that it's usually unnecessary. Experiment and find what works best for you. Count backward starting from ten. I like to say "[step number], going deeper" or "[step number], deeper still" after each step. It helps me go inward and relax my mind faster.

You can even use the staircase method to induce a trance and go into hypnosis. This visual induction is powerful because imagining going down elicits a trance by itself. When doing so, I encourage you to make the images in your mind as vivid and detailed as possible.

Key Steps

- Keep your eyes closed after the induction.
- Imagine a staircase going down.
- With each step, feel yourself going deeper into your unconscious. Count backward and say "[step number], deeper still."
- Optionally, visualize your mind getting darker and quieter as you descend.
- Ten steps is usually enough; twenty at most.

How Does Hypnosis Feel?

One question that often comes up is: "How will I know if I'm actually in hypnosis?" The truth is, hypnosis doesn't feel like being knocked out or losing control. It's usually much more ordinary and comfortable than people expect. You remain aware, able to move and swallow if you need to, and outside sounds may still register in the background. What changes is your focus, you become more absorbed in your inner world, and suggestions are easier to follow.

Some common experiences in trance include:

- A sense of heaviness or lightness in the body.
- Breathing naturally slows down and deepens.

- Warmth, tingling, or gentle waves of comfort.
- A narrowing of focus, with eyes feeling relaxed or fluttering slightly under the lids.
- Time distortion (minutes can feel much shorter or much longer).
- Drifting attention: you may notice images, memories, or just spacious calm.
- Hearing sounds but caring less about them.
- Subtle signs of relaxation such as natural swallows, small twitches (for example, eyelid fluttering is very common) or a sense of stillness.
- A natural reluctance for the eyes to open because it feels more comfortable for them to remain closed.

Sometimes hypnosis feels obvious and deep; other times it's subtle. Both are perfectly valid. What matters is not how dramatic it feels, but whether your unconscious mind is responding. You'll know you're in hypnosis when you notice yourself following your own suggestions more easily, feeling calmer, or sensing a shift in perspective. You'll soon discover that hypnosis feels very comfortable and relaxing.

In hypnosis, you are always safe, always in control, and your unconscious mind will naturally bring you back when it's time. With practice, you'll discover your own personal "flavor" of trance, and it will usually become easier and quicker each time.

Can You Get Stuck in Hypnosis?

People often ask, "Can I get stuck in hypnosis?" The answer is absolutely not. This is a myth. In the entire history of hypnosis, no one has ever been stuck in a trance.

There's a famous story about Milton H. Erickson, a brilliant American psychiatrist who specialized in medical hypnosis and family therapy. At a conference, a presenter had hypnotized a subject who seemed unwilling, or perhaps too comfortable, to come out of trance. Erickson walked calmly onto the stage, leaned down, and whispered something in her ear. She immediately opened her eyes and returned to full awareness.

What did he say?

I know you're so comfortable, so comfortable that you've been in this state for a long time. Soon, your body will have to urinate, and you wouldn't want the embarrassment of doing that in front of all these people, would you?

And just like that, she came back.

The truth is that hypnosis is a safe, comfortable, and calming state. Your unconscious mind, which is you, has always been with you, and it only wants what's best for you. It will never go against your self-protection or body's needs. Entering trance simply gives you a way to harness your unconscious mind's power in a focused way.

All hypnosis is self-hypnosis. You are always the one choosing to go into trance, and you are always in control. So you can trust yourself, relax into the process, and let your unconscious mind work for you.

Key Points

- You cannot get stuck in hypnosis.
- Hypnosis is safe, comfortable, and calming.
- Your unconscious mind always acts in your best interest.

- All hypnosis is self-hypnosis: you are in control.

First Variation: Let the Unconscious Lead

In the first variation of self-hypnosis, we simply enter trance and let the unconscious mind take over. You've already set your intention during the pre-hypnosis step, so now you just allow the process to unfold.

One of the beautiful things about this approach is that your unconscious will automatically deepen the trance for you. It knows exactly how deep you need to go in order to complete the work you've instructed it to do. You don't have to consciously manage the process, your unconscious has been guiding you your entire life, and it understands how to create the right conditions for change.

That said, you can also choose to do the deepening yourself by using the staircase method, and then hand over the reins to your unconscious. Some people enjoy combining the two: consciously deepening first, and then letting the unconscious take them the rest of the way. I encourage you to experiment with both approaches, have fun with it, and see what feels most natural and effective for you.

While in a trance, your unconscious mind will do the work, simply enjoy whatever arises. You might find yourself thinking about something, or nothing at all. You might see images, recall memories, or simply notice sensations in your body. Your mind may drift in and out of focus and that's perfectly fine. Your unconscious knows exactly what to do. I personally enjoy seeing different colors dancing in a wonderful display. I often set this expectation in the pre-step; why not make the experience as enjoyable as possible.

When the time is up, you will naturally return to full awareness. If it helps, you can set a timer, but with practice, you'll often find yourself coming back at just the right moment without one.

Key Steps

- Complete the pre-hypnosis step.
- Do the induction.
- Either let your unconscious deepen the trance for you, or consciously deepen first and then hand over control.
- Let your unconscious guide the process.
- Allow yourself to return naturally or use a timer.

Second Variation: Directing the Work

The second variation starts the same way: you do the pre-hypnosis step, use Breathing With the Eyes or whatever induction feels most natural to you, and allow yourself to drop into trance. The difference is that instead of letting your unconscious run the entire process, you take a more active role and guide the work yourself.

Once you're in that deeper state, you can use one of the transformational techniques I'll teach you in this chapter, such as the Timeline process or Ego State work. These methods allow you to address specific goals, change perceptions, and release patterns that no longer serve you.

When you've completed the work, you reverse the deepening process. If you imagined a staircase going down, imagine walking back up, step by step. With each step, count upward from one to ten, feel yourself becoming more alert and present, until you open your eyes and return fully to the room.

Key Steps

- Complete the pre-hypnosis step.
- Use your chosen induction and deepen the trance.
- Apply your chosen technique or process.
- Reverse the deepening (walk back up the stairs).
- Open your eyes and return fully to awareness.

Self-Hypnosis for Sleep

One of my favorite times to use self-hypnosis is right before bed. I lie down and tell myself, "I'm going into trance for twenty minutes. I want to become more confident. Afterward, I will drift into a deep and restful sleep."

I then do an induction and let my unconscious do the rest. The transition into sleep is smooth, peaceful, and deeply restorative.

Key Steps

- Lie down comfortably before bed.
- Set your intention (duration + desired outcome).
- Use your chosen induction.
- Let the trance naturally transition into sleep.

The more you practice self-hypnosis, the easier it becomes. Hypnosis is both a state and a process, and like any skill, it improves with repetition. With time, you'll find you can drop into trance quickly, do powerful work, and return feeling renewed.

Finding and Installing Resources

One of the most exciting things about self-hypnosis is how flexible it is. Once you learn how to guide yourself into trance, the possibilities for what you can work on are almost limitless. They are only limited by your imagination.

That said, self-hypnosis isn't a magic pill. And saying that is not a cop-out, it's just the truth. If I've never picked up a basketball in my life, no amount of hypnosis is going to make me an NBA player next year. But if I already play basketball at college level, and want to improve my skills and my chances to get drafted, self-hypnosis can be a powerful ally. It can boost motivation, accelerate learning, heighten awareness of opportunities and resources, and strengthen the belief system that supports both my abilities and my identity as an athlete.

The unconscious mind is much less restrictive, less critical, and far more flexible than the conscious mind. It's excellent at mapping resources.

In personal development, a resource is really just anything that helps you grow or handle life a little better. It can be something inside you—confidence, resilience, patience, focus—or something outside you, like a book, a mentor, a tool, or even a moment you once witnessed that stuck with you. If it supports you, lifts you up, or nudges you closer to the person you want to become, it counts as a resource. And the beautiful thing is that your unconscious mind is incredibly good at finding these resources for you, even in places you didn't realize you had stored them.

This means, it can take skills, confidence, or abilities you already have in one area of life and transfer them to another area where you need them.

For example, maybe I want to build confidence in my personal relationships. My unconscious already knows that I'm confident at work or when speaking in front of large groups. It can map the confidence I feel in those situations over to my personal life.

But what if I feel I have no confidence in any area? My unconscious mind can still find what I need. It has access to everything I've experienced, read, heard, and observed. Maybe it remembers a character from a book who radiated confidence, or someone I once saw handle a situation with poise. Those impressions are stored in my unconscious mind, ready to be drawn upon. I can even help this process by surrounding myself with confident people or consuming material, such as books, videos, stories that demonstrate the qualities I want to develop. My unconscious mind will store those examples, and when the time comes, it will map them into the right situation for me.

Even more, the unconscious doesn't stop working when we leave trance. Once we give it a task, it will continue scanning the environment for anything useful to help us achieve our goal, making us more attentive and focused on what matters.

There's one important rule when asking your unconscious to find and install resources: **always frame your intention in positive terms.**

If I say, "Help me not be shy," my mind still has to think about shyness first and in doing so, it reinforces it or puts it in focus. Try this: don't think of a pink elephant. What happened? You pictured one, didn't you? Our minds process negatives by first imagining the very thing we don't want and then marking it as unwanted.

That's why I say, "Help me build confidence in my personal relationships," instead of "Help me stop being nervous." **State what you want, not what you don't want.**

Here's a real example from my own practice: I have cerebral palsy, and while I'm very grateful for my ability to walk, I know it can be improved. I've used hypnosis for this before, and I've found that it works best for me as an ongoing maintenance practice. Every so often, I revisit it. I might say to myself during the pre-hypnosis step:

"I'm going into hypnosis for twenty minutes. I want my unconscious to help me walk in a healthy way, safely, comfortably, and in a way that is good for my balance. I want to remember to bend my knees, stand straight, and keep a relaxed posture. When this is done, I'll drift into a wonderful, peaceful sleep."

Then I use an induction such as Breathing With the Eyes, opening my eyes as I inhale, closing them as I exhale, and imagining my eyelids growing heavier and the space around me darker and calmer. After a few breaths, I simply let my unconscious take over and bring me out of trance when the work is done.

For today, I invite you to go into your first hypnotic trance as part of your daily routine. Choose something specific you want to work on, state it in the positive, and let your unconscious mind find and install the resources you need.

Key Steps

- Choose something you want to improve and state it in positive terms.
- Set a timer (optional).
- Complete the pre-hypnosis step (duration, goal, and how you want to feel afterward).
- Do the induction.
- Let your unconscious mind find and map the resources you need.
- Allow it to bring you out of trance naturally.

Daily Routine 23

1. Do the Heart to Yes technique.
2. Practice mindfulness meditation for ten minutes.
3. Journal for five to ten minutes.
4. Choose one thing you'd like to improve. State your intention in positive terms, go into trance, and let your unconscious do the work. For example, you could say something like: "I will go into hypnosis for twenty minutes, I want my unconscious mind to help me focus at work, after which I will feel refreshed and ready to have a great day."
5. Use the following summary to guide you into your first hypnotic trance and let your unconscious mind do the work.

As you read the summary, you might notice that some instructions appear more than once. That's intentional. Repetition helps you absorb and integrate the resources we're exploring together. So be patient with the process, it really does pay off.

Step 1: Pre-Hypnosis—Set Your Intention

Before you close your eyes, decide exactly what you want to work on in trance.

- Be specific. Instead of "I want to feel better," say "I want to feel calm and confident during tomorrow's presentation." Experiment with various degrees of specificity. Being specific will lead to better results in some situations, but it's also useful to let your unconscious mind work on broader transformations, although this might require a longer hypnosis session.
- State it in **positive terms**, focus on what you *do* want, not what you want to avoid.
- Decide how long you'll stay in trance (for example, fifteen or twenty minutes). Set a timer if you'd like.
- Decide how you want to feel afterward: refreshed and energized, or relaxed and ready for sleep.

Think of this as making a contract with yourself, you're giving your unconscious mind a clear job description.

Step 2: Induction—Entering Trance

Use the *Breathing With the Eyes* or any other hypnosis induction.

- Sit or lie down in a safe, quiet space and turn off any device that might distract you. If you tend to fall asleep, sitting is better.
- Pick a point across the room to focus on.
- As you inhale deeply, open your eyes wide as if you're breathing in through them.

- As you exhale, close your eyes slowly, imagining your eyelids are heavy and relaxed.
- Repeat this three to five times, each time letting your eyelids feel heavier.
- On the final exhale, keep your eyes closed.

Step 3: Deepening the Trance—Going Further In

Deepening makes the trance more comfortable and focused. For today's practice, let your unconscious deepen the hypnotic trance for you.

Step 4: The Work—Let Your Unconscious Lead

Once you're in trance, let go. Allow whatever comes to your mind to unfold, enjoy it, and trust your unconscious to do its excellent work. Let the unconscious mind take over. You've already set your intention. Now simply relax and allow whatever happens to happen. Your unconscious knows how deep you need to go and what steps to take. It will do the work for you and bring you back when it's done.

Step 5: Coming Out of Hypnosis—Returning to Full Awareness

- You will simply find yourself naturally returning when the work is complete.
- If you opt for feeling awake and refreshed, as you open your eyes, stretch or move gently before standing. And take a moment to notice how you feel.

Exploring and Changing Your Timeline

In this section, I want to show you how to explore and change your personal timeline. Now, to be clear, I don't mean literally going into the past to change history, or jumping into the future to guarantee a specific outcome. As much as I'd like to do that sometimes, we can't control the past or the future.

What we can control is who we are in the present. Through self-hypnosis, we can work with our brain's perception of time to influence how we see the past, how we imagine the future, and most importantly, how we live right now. Timeline work can completely shift the way we experience life in the present moment.

Locating Your Timeline

Let's start with a little exercise. Close your eyes and imagine yourself standing on the timeline of your life. Where is your past? For many people, it's to the left or behind them. Where is your future? Often, it's in front of them or to the right.

These are just the two most common ways people represent their timelines, but your mind might organize it differently. There's no wrong answer, it's your own construct. If your mental image is unique, that's perfect. And if you can't quite see it at first, don't worry. You might hear it, feel it, or just have a sense of it. Some people's visualization muscles are a little rusty at first. If that's the case, just pretend you can see something and let it develop over time. What we've been studying still applies here: give yourself compassion.

The Purpose of Timeline Work

Once you have an idea of your timeline's layout, you can begin using it as a powerful tool for change. Timeline work is about changing how your brain stores and responds to past and future events which in turn changes how you feel and behave in the present.

You can use Timeline work to:

- Reframe and heal painful memories.
- Prepare for upcoming events with greater confidence and calm and any other feelings you may need.
- Adjust your perception of the road ahead (your timeline) so it feels more supportive and motivating.

Preparing for Timeline Work

The process starts with the four steps of self-hypnosis:

1. **Pre-Hypnosis Step**: Decide what event you want to work on and state your goal in positive terms. For example, "I want to feel confident during my presentation" rather than "I don't want to be nervous."
2. **Induction**: Use one of the inductions to enter trance.
3. **Deepening**: Imagine walking down a staircase, step by step, until you feel deeply relaxed.
4. **The Work**: Apply the Timeline technique to the situation you've chosen.

I personally like to use the second variation of self-hypnosis for Timeline work, where I guide the process as the hypnotist, but you can also allow your unconscious to run the show once you know the steps.

Working with the Past

Once you've completed your induction and deepening, imagine yourself standing on your timeline in the present moment. From there, float above it and gently move toward the past event you want to work on. Go at whatever speed feels right until you arrive at that moment in time.

People perceive these scenes differently, some see them as a movie on a screen, others as a play, and some step right into the memory. *If the emotions feel too intense, create distance by viewing it from farther away or as if you were watching from the audience.*

From this vantage point, you can do powerful work:

- **Coach your younger self**: Acknowledge their hurt and let them know they're safe. Remind them that you now know how things unfold, and they will feel better in time. Ask gentle, useful questions to learn more about the situation and help them discover new insights.
- **Validate their feelings**: Say things like, "It's okay to feel this way. I'm here with you."
- **Transfer resources**: Give them courage, strength, love, or whatever they needed in that moment. You can even visualize hugging them and sending that resource directly into them.

- **Adjust the scene:** Change elements of the environment or add supportive people to make the moment feel safer.

When the work feels complete, float forward along your timeline to moments just after the event and notice how things feel. You can even drift into your imagined future to explore how this shift may influence what comes next. If the change feels right, keep it. If not, return to the event and continue refining.

An Example: Comforting a Younger Self

Here's an example of how this can look in practice.

Imagine you want to work on the grief of losing someone you loved. You set your intention before the session: "I want this session to bring me comfort over losing my uncle."

After floating back to that moment in time, you might choose to speak to your younger self. They didn't have the tools you have today. You might say, "I know how sad you are right now, and it's okay. I'm here with you."

You could give them resilience by embracing them and letting that courage flow into them. This becomes even more effective if you act out the hug with your body. It might sound simple or silly, but it's deeply comforting and can be life-changing.

Sometimes comfort isn't enough, and the scene itself needs to shift. **Ask your younger self what they need.** If they wish a supportive person had been there, imagine bringing that person in. If they'd feel better without someone who was present, remove that person. You can also adjust the details:

brighten a rainy day, change the setting, or alter their clothing so they feel stronger and safer. Small changes can make a big difference. *I highly recommend having an open conversation with your younger self; this helps you discover what they truly need so you can support them accurately and compassionately.*

Working with the Future

You don't have to start in the past, you can work with the future too. For example, maybe you have a big presentation coming up. After the induction and deepening, you can move forward along your timeline to the moment of the presentation.

From there, notice how your future self is feeling. If they seem anxious, give them the confidence, calm, and focus they need. You can also visit moments leading up to the event, days or weeks ahead, to help your future self prepare, rehearse, and build momentum. This is very empowering.

In this way, you're coaching yourself forward in time, ensuring you arrive at that moment ready and resourced.

Adjusting the Present Perspective

Sometimes you might choose to remain in the present on your timeline, simply looking ahead and noticing the road before you. If it appears narrow, dark, or bumpy, you can widen it, smooth it, or add lights. Maybe you plant trees, add open spaces, or replace tall, imposing skyscrapers with cozy houses.

Even if these changes seem symbolic, your unconscious mind understands their meaning and will act on it. In the coming chapter on Visualization++, you'll learn more about how we can use our sensory systems to change the way we perceive reality and how we feel about our past, present and future.

The Beauty of Timeline Work

This process is incredibly flexible. You can start in the past, the future, or the present. You can work with events directly, coach versions of yourself, or simply change the symbolic structure of your timeline. Each approach can shift how your brain stores experiences, which changes how you feel and how you show up in everyday life.

While I've done Timeline work by letting my unconscious take the lead, I usually get the best results when I guide the process myself using the second variation of self-hypnosis. That said, both approaches can be valuable. Experiment and see which works best for you.

Key Steps for Timeline Work

1. Set your intention in the pre-hypnosis step (state it positively).
2. Use an induction to go into trance.
3. Deepen the trance with the staircase method.
4. Locate your timeline (past, present, future).
5. Float above it to gain perspective.
6. Move to the moment you want to work on.
7. Transform the scene, coach yourself, or add/remove symbolic elements.
8. Check the changes by moving forward in time.
9. Return to the present and come out of trance.

In the next section, I'll share a real example of me using self-hypnosis and Timeline work on myself. This is not a script for you to follow step-by-step, but it will give you a clear picture of what's possible and how this process looks in real life.

Example of Timeline Work on Myself

I want to give you a real, **unfiltered** example of how I use self-hypnosis with Timeline work on myself. As I mentioned earlier, this isn't meant to be a script for you to follow, it's simply me letting you into my own process so you can see what it really looks like in practice.

In the original session, I spoke out loud so you could hear my inner dialogue, which means I wasn't in as deep a trance as I would normally go. But even so, the emotions and insights I was able to tap into were real and deeply healing. This is a polished transcript of the recording.

Let's begin.

I'm going to go into hypnosis for about ten minutes.
I want to work on my past experience with bullying.
I want to feel supported, and I want to be able to take different actions so that, in my life now, I will feel more confident, more valuable.

When this is done, I'll come out of trance feeling refreshed, full of energy, and ready to go on with the rest of my day.

[Using the Breathing With the Eyes induction]

I visualize the staircase and go down step by step.
As I go down, I imagine my mind becoming more and more relaxed... going deeper.
It's a staircase, and I'm going down. My unconscious mind knows exactly where I need to be to do the work.

Step by step... darker... deeper... further into my unconscious.

I go down a second staircase.
I feel comfortable, at ease.
Deeper still.

Now I imagine I'm standing on my timeline.
The future is in front of me.
The past is behind me.

I float above the timeline and move toward one of the first events I can remember being bullied.

I see myself, I am maybe six or seven years old, with a nervous smile.
I'm nervous to go to school. That's okay.
I tell my younger self: "I know you're nervous. I'm here with you."

We're on the bus.
It's not the first time I've ridden it; I know the people.
There's this bigger kid.
He calls me a name.

It's silly but to me, it's not silly. He says "Jean-FranFOU", which means "Jean-FranCrazy."

I don't remember if I cried, but I remember it hurt.

I tell my younger self: "Yes, it did hurt. And it's okay to cry if you want."
I ask: "Would you like me to sit with you?"
He says yes.

I sit with him.
I ask: "Do you want me to talk to the big guy?"
He says yes.

So I turn to the kid and, very gently, I explain how it can hurt little Jean-François, and that I'd appreciate it if he stopped.

Then I turn back to my younger self and say: "Even if he says that, you know it doesn't mean it's true, right?"

He thinks for a moment. Then says: "But I think it is true."

I ask: "Why do you think that?"

He says: "Because he knows better than me."

I say: "Why do you think he knows better than you?"

He says: "Because he's older."

So I tell him: "Well... if being older means knowing better, then I'm older than you, right?"

He nods.

"Then let me tell you, he doesn't know better than you. Maybe he knows some things, but that doesn't mean what he said is true. I believe you're not crazy. I believe you deserve to be treated better."

I ask: "Would you like a hug?"
He says yes.

I hug him and say: "I'm going to give you some courage to help you say 'please stop' next time, but also the courage to know that even if they don't stop, you're still valuable. You're still not crazy. You're smart. You're courageous. People love you and people will love you in your future. You will do great things. And never let go of the love you have for yourself and for other people. Even when they're mean. You can always walk away, you don't have to take it. But you can do that with gentleness and love."

I ask: "Is there anything else I can help you with today?"
He says: "Can you remove my disability?"

I say: "I'm sorry, I can't do that. But I can tell you your future is a good one. Keep persevering. Keep giving yourself gentleness, love, and patience. You are exceptional. You deserve to be loved. And your disability doesn't take any of that away from you. I love you."

Now I rise above the timeline and move forward, but still in my past, toward a big bullying event in high school.

I drop down into the scene.
Someone slaps me in the face. My glasses go flying.
At the time, I tried to hit him back. And after that, he never bothered me again.

But I know that moment left me with a bit of a fight response.

So I replay it.
This time, right before he hits me, I step back.

I look him in the eye and say: "I know you're doing this because you're hurting. I know you have problems at home. I'm sorry, that must be really hard. But I do not want you to touch me, try to touch me, or tease me ever again. Is that understood?"

He says "yes."
He even says "sorry."

I float forward in time and see that he never bothers me again.
A little further forward, I see that I'm more gentle with my own kids.

I keep moving forward, past the present, and notice that in situations where I might feel bullied, it feels different.
I have value.
I can stand up for myself without aggression.
I feel compassion for myself and others.

I embrace my future self and integrate these new insights.
I say thank you.

I float back to the present and see stairs leading up.
I go up the first level. Then the second.

It gets brighter.
I start to wiggle my fingers.
Feel my body.

And I come out energized, happy.

I didn't expect to get so emotional.
Honestly, I thought I wouldn't go into a deep trance because I was speaking out loud for you. But I did. Maybe not as deep as usual, but it was a fantastic trance. And I got very emotional, I wasn't acting.

I chose something I thought wouldn't be too intense. But clearly, there was still something there. And I'm glad you witnessed it because it doesn't get more real than this.

The way I feel right now… calm, grounded, and very aware that I am okay. I am loved.

Reflections After the Session

Even when I was speaking out loud for this demonstration and staying partly aware of the *outside world*, the work still went surprisingly deep. I didn't expect to get emotional, but the process brought things up I didn't realize were still there, and that's part of the beauty of Timeline work: we can uncover and shift things we didn't consciously plan for. Sometimes we might choose to fully step into our younger self and experience the scene as if we are living it again; other times, we might stay more distant and observe, which can make intense moments easier to work with.

You don't have to begin with a deeply traumatic event, starting with something lighter will still bring meaningful change. In the end, the real power of this process isn't just in changing how you relate to your past or how you prepare for the future, it's in how grounded, supported, and at peace you feel in the present afterward.

I instructed my unconscious to go into hypnosis for about ten minutes and it ended up being much longer. Honestly, even though I said "ten minutes," I was expecting it might be closer to twenty. That's because my unconscious mind knew the work that had to be done, I trusted it to take me there and bring me back at the right time.

You may want to set an alarm to make sure you don't miss something in your schedule, but when possible, I encourage you to do this work when you have the time to let it run its full course. Don't rush. This work is important, and you deserve to do it to completion.

Key Points from This Example

- **Set a clear, positive intention** before starting. Focus on what you *want* to feel or achieve, not what you want to avoid.
- **Use the induction and deepening** steps to fully enter trance before beginning the Timeline work.
- **Float to the chosen point on your timeline**: past, present, or future, and view the event from a safe, comfortable perspective.
- **Engage with your younger or future self**: offer comfort, reassurance, skills, or resources.
- **Alter the scene if needed**: change the environment, add supportive people, or remove harmful ones.
- **Check the ripple effects** by moving forward on the timeline to see how the changes influence later events.
- **Integrate the new insights** before returning to the present and coming out of trance. This can be done by hugging or by imagining a beam of light between you and your past or future self.
- Remember: **you control the depth and intensity**. You can step back from the scene at any time if it feels overwhelming.
- **Be gentle with yourself**, don't take on too much at first. As you practice, you will discover new ways and tools to help you transform your mind and life.

You are now ready to practice Timeline work on yourself. For the next two days, I invite you to set aside at least twenty minutes each day to do Timeline work on yourself.

Daily Routine 24 & 25

1. Do the Heart to Yes technique.
2. Practice mindfulness meditation for ten minutes.
3. Journal for five to ten minutes.
4. In the next two days, find a situation from your past in which you feel you would appreciate being given a different perspective, help and comfort and apply the Timeline technique while in a trance. To do so, use the second variation of self-hypnosis, and follow these four simple steps:

Step 1: Pre-Hypnosis—Set Your Intention

Before you go in a trance, decide exactly what you want to work on in trance.

- Be specific. Instead of "I want to fix my past," say "I want my unconscious mind to help me find peace about the bullying experiences I had as a kid"
- State it in **positive terms**: focus on what you *do* want and not what you want to avoid.
- Decide how long you'll stay in trance (I recommend twenty minutes).
- Decide how you want to feel afterward: refreshed and energized, or relaxed and ready for sleep.

Step 2: Induction—Entering Trance

You'll use the Breathing With the Eyes or your favorite induction.

- Sit or lie down in a safe, quiet space and turn off your mobile devices. If you tend to fall asleep, sitting is better.
- Pick a point across the room to focus on.
- As you inhale deeply, open your eyes wide as if you're breathing in through them.
- As you exhale, close your eyes slowly, imagining your eyelids are heavy and relaxed.
- Repeat this three to five times, each time letting your eyelids feel heavier.
- On the final exhale, keep your eyes closed.

Step 3: Deepening the Trance—Going Further In

Deepening makes the trance more comfortable and easier to maintain.

- Imagine a staircase in front of you.
- With each step down, count backward from ten to one, feeling yourself going deeper into your unconscious mind.
- You might imagine it getting darker, quieter, or more peaceful as you descend.
- I invite you to go down a second set of stairs for these sessions.

Step 4: The Work—You Lead the Session

Once you're in trance, gently instruct your unconscious mind to locate your personal timeline. Float above it and move to the point (past, present, or future) you want to work on. From there, transform the scene: coach your past or future self, add resources, or adjust symbolic elements like light, color, or environment. Test the change by moving forward along the timeline, then return to the present when you're satisfied.

Step 5: Coming Out of Hypnosis—Returning to Full Awareness

- You used the staircase method for deepening the trance, now imagine walking back up, step by step, becoming more alert with each number, from one to ten.
- If your intent is to feel awake and refreshed, when you open your eyes, stretch or move gently before standing. Take a moment to notice how you feel.

Remember to be gentle with yourself. When coaching your past or your future self, do so with gentleness, compassion and love as if you were talking to your best friend.

Healing Your Ego States

Now let's dive into the second transformational technique you'll use with the second variation of self-hypnosis.

Ego states, often called parts, were first identified by Paul Federn, and many others have since expanded on the concept. One of my favorite modern resources is Gordon Emmerson's book on Ego State Therapy. It's approachable, practical, and an excellent choice if you want to explore this work more deeply.

An ego state is simply a part of you, a version of yourself that formed around certain experiences, emotions, or needs. We all have many of these inner parts. Some are confident, some are protective, and some carry old hurts. By understanding and working with these parts, we can create more clarity, healing, and inner alignment.

It's said that we each have somewhere between 100 and 150 ego states. Not all of them are active at once, most of the time we regularly use only five to fifteen in our daily lives. Imagine your mind as a large ship. The ego states you use day-to-day are like the crew members working on the main deck: they're visible, active, and taking turns steering the ship. The rest of your ego states are below deck, not gone, just quieter. They mostly stay out of sight until they're needed or triggered, carrying their own roles, skills, and stories.

At any given time, one part is at the helm, meaning it's executive, it's the one in control of your thoughts, feelings, and behavior in that moment. That part could be a confident public speaker, a nurturing caregiver, a cautious protector, or a self-doubting critic. All of them are you, they just have different functions. Sometimes, the executive part—in command of the ship—is not equipped, doesn't have the proper dynamics with other parts or is the wrong choice to handle the current situation.

The ego state work we explore in this chapter will help create more internal alignment and reduce situations like this.

Why Is Ego State Work Powerful?

Working with ego states in hypnosis is powerful because we communicate directly with the part of us that holds a particular belief, feeling, or habit. We help that part feel safe, supported, and understood. Sometimes we help it take on a new role; other times we mediate between parts so they work together instead of being in conflict.

But to do this well, there are a few essential guidelines we must follow. These make the work more respectful, effective, and sustainable.

Core Principles for Ego State Work

When working with ego states, the most important thing to remember is that **each part is a valuable and well-intentioned aspect of you**. Even if a part's current behavior feels unhelpful, it developed to serve a purpose, often to protect you in some way. This is why **the first principle is to always approach each part with gentleness and compassion**. Your role is not to fight with it or push it away, but to understand it, make it feel safe, and let it know you're here to help.

Any time we want to work with a part, we invite it to become executive, the part in control for that moment, so we can directly interact with it. From there, we ask its name, age, and role or job within our inner world. *This opens the door to trust and collaboration.* If we want to suggest a change, whether in its behavior, role, or relationship to other parts, we always ask how it feels about that suggestion. **Consent is essential.** If a part isn't ready to change, we negotiate and adapt until we find a way forward that works for all parts.

Ego state work also involves helping our parts support each other. With permission, we introduce them, encourage dialogue, and connect a struggling part with others that hold useful resources. Before we end a session, it's important to check in with all parts to ensure there's consensus on the work done. If a part has objections, we take the time to hear them out and address their concerns. This respect for every voice within us is what makes Ego State work so powerful and so healing.

Key Points

1. **Be gentle**: Approach each part with gratitude, compassion, patience, and kindness.

2. **Make them feel safe**: Let them know you're there to help, not judge or push them away.
3. **Invite them to be executive**: Before speaking with a part, ask it to step forward and take control for the moment.
4. **Ask their name, age, and job**: Understanding who they are and what role they play helps build trust and clarity.
5. **Seek permission before change**: When you want to suggest a change, ask how they feel about it and negotiate if needed.
6. **Facilitate cooperation**: You can invite parts to talk to each other or seek help from other parts but always ask for permission.
7. **Reach consensus**: Before ending the session, ask all parts if they're comfortable with the work done. If a part objects, work with it until you find common ground.

The Role of the Higher Self

In this model, one special part helps coordinate the others. Often called the Inner Strength or Higher Self, this part has been with you your entire life and is respected by all other parts. It's usually the same age as you and acts as a wise, unifying presence. When there's disagreement between parts, your Higher Self can help bring everyone together toward a shared goal.

The Heart of the Work

At its core, Ego State work is a conversation with yourself, just as we explored in the Timeline process. Every part is you. Every part acts with a positive intention, even if its strategy is outdated or unhelpful now. Our job is to acknowledge that intention, update the role if needed, and create better cooperation among all parts of ourselves.

This might mean helping a part take on a new and more supportive job; one that serves you better in your life now than the role it originally adopted. Sometimes, this involves transforming the way the part appears to you, so its image reflects its new function or energy. You might also encourage it to partner with other parts, creating a sense of teamwork and shared purpose. In some cases, the part may even choose a new name or identity that better matches its updated role, symbolising the shift it's made.

Key Strategies for Helping Parts

- Giving a part a new, more helpful job.
    - Discuss with the ego state to help them find a new job that will use their skills and serve you better.
- Transforming the way it appears.
    - Ask them if they would like a new outfit. Often changing their appearance will help them adopt a new role: a new identity.
- Helping it partner with other parts.
    - Invite them to talk to other parts to find a solution, a common ground, and report back to you. Give them time to do so. Time of silence in Ego State work is powerful and essential.
- Changing its name and identity to match its new role.

- Ask them if they would like a new name. This helps the part step into their new identity and feel proud.

When we do this respectfully, the impact can be profound. I've seen it in clients, and I've experienced it in my own life.

In the next section, I'll share a real example of me using self-hypnosis to work with my own ego states. This isn't a step-by-step script for you to follow exactly, but rather a glimpse into how the process looks and feels in practice, so you can see the depth and transformation this work can offer.

Example of Ego State Work on Myself

In this section, I'm going to share something deeply personal, a real example of me using self-hypnosis and Ego State work on myself.

This isn't a shortened demonstration or a clean, perfect script. What you're about to read is essentially a faithful transcript of an actual self-hypnosis session I recorded for myself. You'll notice there's repetition, pauses, little tangents, and natural rephrasing, and that's not a mistake. It's exactly how real unconscious work happens.

Sometimes a part needs to hear something several times before it lands. Sometimes I circle back to a point in a different way so the meaning can sink in. These repetitions aren't inefficiency, they're part of how deep change works.

I'm sharing it with you as-is so you can witness the feel of a genuine, in-the-moment self-hypnosis session. This way, when you do it yourself, you'll know it doesn't have to be perfectly scripted or linear to be deeply effective.

Setting the Intention

I'm going to go into a trance for about twenty minutes. My goal today is to work with my unconscious through Ego State work to build more confidence in my personal relationships, especially romantic ones.

I want to feel valued. I want to feel confident. I want to be at ease, be witty, and stay fully aware of the other person. I want to be self-aware of how I'm feeling, and I want to be authentic.

When I come out of trance, I want to feel fantastic, energized, happy, and ready for anything.

Induction and Deepening

[Using the Breathing With the Eyes induction]

I imagine a staircase going down. I start to walk down, step by step.

As I go, I imagine my mind becoming darker: less light, more comfort. I imagine going more and more into my unconscious, one step at a time.

When I reach the bottom of one level, I decide to go down one more.

I go deeper, into a place of comfort, a place where I can change many aspects of my life in a powerful, positive way.

Calling the Higher Self

I ask to speak with the part of myself that identifies as my Higher Self.

"When you're ready to talk," I say inside my mind, "just come and say, 'I'm here.'"

Higher Self: "I'm here."

Myself: "Thank you, Higher Self. Can I talk to you and call you Higher Self?"

Higher Self: "Yes."

Myself: "Thank you. I'd like your help building more confidence with my relationships, especially romantic relationships. I want to feel confident, to be able to talk to romantic prospects, people I could have a relationship with, and be confident, know my value, and have fun doing it. Could you help me with that?"

Higher Self: "Yes, of course."

Identifying Another Part

Myself: "Do you know if there are any parts that would need help with me being more confident in that context?"

Higher Self: "Yes."

Myself: "Could you tell me which parts?"

Higher Self: "Yes."

Myself: "What is that part called?"

Higher Self: "It's called the Disabled Part."

Speaking to the Disabled Part

Myself: "Okay, thank you. Do you mind if I go talk to that part?"

Higher Self: "No."

Myself: "Disabled Part, if you don't mind, I'd like to talk to you. Just let me know when you're ready."

Disabled Part: "I'm here."

Myself: "Thank you. We want to be more confident in romantic relationships. Can you let me know how you feel about that?"

Disabled Part: "I feel very self-conscious. I feel that... I don't deserve to be in a relationship."

Myself: "Thank you for sharing. Can you tell me why that is? Remember, I'm here to help you. I want what's best for you."

Disabled Part: "I think I'm embarrassed that I don't look the same way as other people. I cannot do the same things. I don't talk the same way. I feel like I will be a burden on someone who could be romantic with me."

Myself: "Thank you for sharing. Can you think of anything that I or other parts could help you with, something that would help you feel you deserve to be in a relationship and that you won't be a burden?"

Disabled Part: "I'm not sure. I also feel like it's my fault that our relationship with our ex ended."

Consulting the Higher Self

Myself: "That's interesting, thank you for sharing that. Can we go talk to the Higher Self part together, just to discuss what you've said and see if they can offer a little advice or comfort?"

Disabled Part: "Yes, please. I'd love that."

Myself : "Thank you. Higher Self, when you're ready to talk to us, please come and say, 'I'm here.'"

Higher Self: "I'm here."

Myself: "So, the Disabled Part feels like they will be a burden on the romantic person. They feel self-conscious about how they look, how they talk, how they walk and how they're different. Do you have anything that could help the Disabled Part feel better about this?"

Higher Self: "Yes, Jean-François. I know it can be very difficult because we didn't choose to be this way. But I want to say that without you, the Disabled Part, we wouldn't be who we are.

You have done many things that are beneficial for us. You have helped us with perseverance, with learning what it means to persevere. You have helped us take time to do things. You've helped us learn to accept help from others.

You've also helped us stand out. Sometimes you don't like it, but you are very different from other people, and that makes you stand out, and a lot of the time, in a good way.

I know it doesn't take away the fact that you feel different, and that sometimes it's been very hard to accept all the challenges you bring as being a disabled person. And I know that in the past we've been very closed to the idea of accepting that, yes, we are different. There are a lot of things we don't have a choice over.

But it's also good to accept that everyone in the whole world has things they feel different about. And for some of them, they might have a choice, but for many they really don't, just like you.

And I want to give you compassion right now. It's okay to feel different. It's okay to feel pissed off sometimes that you can't do things that other people can do. It's okay to be scared. It's okay to be angry.

But you need to realize that other people have limits too. And that doesn't take away your limits, it just puts it in perspective."

Disabled Part: "There's also something else that bothers me. I've heard so many times when I was younger that 'it's okay that you're disabled because you bring so much more… you have so many better qualities that make up for your disability.' And that always put so much pressure on me."

Myself: "Thank you for sharing. I really appreciate that."

Inviting the Compassion Part

Myself: "I feel there might be other parts that could help us with this."

Compassion: "Yes, I'm here."

Myself: "Okay, what do I call you?"

Compassion: "Compassion."

Myself: "You seem eager right now."

Compassion: "Yes, I'm eager because I know we've been really harsh in the past, and I want to take more space as the Compassion Part.

I want to comfort the Disabled Part. I want to say that you don't have to be perfect. We don't have to be perfect because we have a disability. We are allowed to make mistakes. We are allowed not to always be in a good mood. We are allowed to not always be motivated or motivating.

That's what it is to be human. We are not perfect. And not only do we need to know that, we need to accept it and live by it.

Don't worry, it's not an excuse, it's just reality. And I want to encourage you and **enable** you to remember that.

All of the parts, including you, Disabled Part, are you okay with giving yourself more compassion?"

Disabled Part: "Yes, I want to."

Compassion: "And remember, you don't have to be perfect at it. Just do your best to give compassion to Jean-François."

Myself: "Thank you, Compassion Part, for helping us. Thank you, Higher Self. And thank you, Disabled Part, for helping."

Name Change and New Identity

Myself: "Disabled Part, is there anything else you'd like us to do today to help you feel more confident in romantic relationships?"

Disabled Part: "I'd like to accept my part in our separation from our ex, but also let go of everything that's not my fault. And

I would like the other parts to do the same, if they can agree to that."

Myself: "Thank you, Disabled Part. Can you go and ask all the other parts if they're okay with your suggestion?"

[After a brief moment]

Disabled Part: "Yes, they are."

Myself: "Thank you. And thank the other parts for me."

"Now, is there anything else we can do for you, Disabled Part? Maybe change your name, if you'd like, or change the way you look?"

Disabled Part: "I'd like to keep part of the name because now I feel like I play an important role. But I'd like to add something to it."

Myself: "Okay, go ahead."

Disabled Part: "I'd like to be known as the Disabled Tiger to represent that, yes, I'm disabled, but I still have strength, and I've built a lot of resilience over the years in my role."

Myself: "Thank you, Disabled Tiger. I appreciate that."

Inviting the Confidence Part

Myself: "Is there any other part that would like to help with building confidence in a romantic relationship? If so, just come and say your name."

Confidence: "Yes, I'm Confidence."

Myself: "Hey, Confidence. Thank you. How would you like to help?"

Confidence: "I'd like to help the Timid Part, the Unsure Part, to feel like it's okay to try new things. It's okay to dare and talk to women. They're just other human beings. And it's okay to try and fail. Failure is how we learn. That's how we grow our skills: talking to people.

It's also how we learn about ourselves, by learning what we like, what we don't like.

I'd like to offer a mindset we've been using at work with Jean-François. Instead of going to an interview thinking: Oh man... will they like me? Will they hire me? Go in thinking: Do I like them? Do I want to work with them? Do I want to be here?

Let's integrate that for romantic relationships. Don't go in harshly evaluating people, that's not what I mean. But have fun. See if there's a connection. See if that person likes your Disabled Tiger, with everything that comes with it.

See if it's a good fit. And if it's not, it's not against you. It just means they need someone different.

That's the process and mindset I'd like to suggest when you go talk to people, especially in your romantic endeavors."

Meeting the Timid Part

Myself: "Thank you, Confidence Part. Can you go and ask all the other parts if they agree with this?"

Timid: "Hey, I'm Timid. I'm the only part that's not sure about this."

Myself: "Okay, thank you, Timid. What are you not sure about?"

Timid: "I'm scared. I'm scared I'll be rejected."

Myself: "That's understandable. How could we help you with this?"

Timid: "I want to know that we can take it. I want to know that being rejected won't sink us into a deep hole where we'll be depressed."

Myself: "Okay, that's totally fair. And I don't think any other part wants that, right? Is there anything, Timid, that we can change about your appearance that could help you feel better?"

Timid: "I'd like a suit."

Myself: "Okay. What colour?"

Timid: "A fancy dark grey suit. And I want to stand tall."

Myself: "Go ahead, do that for yourself."

Strengthening Timid with Support

Myself: "Thank you for doing that. How do you feel now?"

Timid: "A little bit better. I'd like to be closer to the Higher Self because I know the Higher Self can support us so we don't feel depressed after rejection."

Higher Self: "Of course. I'd like to remind the Timid Part that failure can be seen as learning. I'm happy to repeat that and coach the Timid Part on this."

Myself: "What do you think, Timid Part? Does that make sense?"

Timid: "Yes, thank you."

Consensus

Myself: "Okay, so now are we all in agreement? Higher Self, can you check with all the parts and make sure we all agree that to be confident in our romantic relationships, we can do all these modifications and keep them?"

[After a brief moment]

Higher Self: "Yes, we're all okay."

Myself: "Okay. I want to thank you, Higher Self. I want to thank Disabled Tiger. Thank you, Confidence Part. Thank you, Timid Part. Thank you, all of you. Thank you for letting me help you."

Returning to Full Awareness

Now I'm coming back, walking up the stairs, taking all the work we've done with me as I go up, knowing that it is here to stay. I trust my parts.

I've done excellent work.

Now I walk up even more... oh, feeling great.

Reflections After the Session

This one was less emotional than the Timeline work example. I think it's because I've already done a fair bit of work around this issue before, so there were fewer surprises. Also, I did this right after a deep session of Timeline work, and these processes build on each other. Even when they focus on different parts or issues, they add up. Every bit of work we do in hypnosis multiplies, shaping the life we want and helping us know ourselves better.

There are always surprises, though. Sometimes I discover a part I didn't know was still active, or I find a new angle on something I've worked with before. What strikes me every time is how much gentleness, compassion, and respect are embedded in this process. Even when a part resists, like my Timid Part did in this session, that's just an opening for collaboration. With a little creativity (in this case, giving it a suit and support from the Higher Self), we can help every part feel safe and valued.

That's the heart of Ego State work: a real, respectful conversation with yourself, where every part has a voice, every part belongs, and change happens through understanding, not force.

Key Points

- **Set a clear intention**: Decide exactly what you want to work on before starting your trance.
- **Invite the Higher Self first**: Begin by calling forward your Higher Self to guide the process and coordinate other parts.
- **Ask which parts need attention**: Let your Higher Self identify the parts most involved with your goal.
- **Work gently and respectfully**: Approach each part with compassion, understanding their positive intention, even if their current behavior seems unhelpful.

- **Ask for consent before change**: Always check how a part feels about making changes and be willing to negotiate.
- **Encourage cooperation between parts**: Invite parts to support each other, share resources, or work together toward the goal.
- **Offer transformation options**: A part can change its role, appearance, name, or identity to reflect its new function.
- **Address resistance directly**: If a part is hesitant, explore its concerns, find supportive solutions, and involve the Higher Self when needed.
- **Confirm group agreement**: Before ending, ensure all parts agree to the new changes and are comfortable moving forward.
- **Return with integration**: Bring the findings, insights and changes back with you as you come out of trance, trusting they will stay with you.

How Often Should You Practice Self-Hypnosis?

Self-hypnosis is one of the most powerful tools we have for transforming our lives, and the more we use it, the easier and more natural it becomes. It can help us build new and empowering habits, replace limiting beliefs with useful ones, process difficult emotions in a healthy way, sharpen skills in sports, the arts, public speaking, relationships, or at work, and improve focus, concentration, and even reading speed. The only real limitation is our imagination and even that can be expanded by using self-hypnosis to become more creative.

At one point in my own life, I experienced waves of deep sadness about something that had happened between me and a romantic partner. It was difficult to focus and feel grounded. I decided to go into trance for ten to twenty minutes with the specific intention that my unconscious mind would process the emotion in a way that left me calmer, more stable, and more at peace and without repressing any of my feelings. I also told myself that when I came out of trance, I would feel refreshed, energized, and ready to continue my day. And that's exactly what happened. I could have used Timeline work or Ego State work to address it, and both would have been effective, but I wanted to show myself how simple it can be to give our unconscious the task and let it do the work.

You can use self-hypnosis as often as you want. In fact, I recommend practicing it daily at first, so the process becomes second nature. Think of it as another powerful tool in your self-care and self-mastery toolkit. You can use it to process emotions, create new habits, rehearse skills, reframe experiences, or shape your mindset. One of my favorite ways to use it is to fall asleep. This is a great way to get regular practice while drifting off quickly and easily.

We've only scratched the surface of what's possible with hypnosis in this chapter, but that's more than enough for you to begin doing amazing work on yourself.

Stay curious.

Experiment.

Discover what works best for you, and don't be afraid to adapt the techniques to fit your style. If you want to go deeper into hypnosis and self-hypnosis, I highly recommend looking into Mike Mandel Hypnosis. Mike Mandel and Chris Thompson are incredible hypnotists, gifted teachers, and a lot of fun to learn from. You now have a tool that can help you process, change, and grow every single day. Use it frequently and see how it transforms your life.

For the next two days, I invite you to put this into action. Choose a specific skill you'd like to improve or a behavior you want to change, something meaningful, but manageable enough to explore in a short session. Once you've decided, use self-hypnosis to enter a trance and apply the Ego State technique you've learned. Engage directly with the parts of yourself that influence this skill or behavior, working with them to create new roles, perspectives, or strategies that will support your growth. This focused practice will not only move you closer to your goal, it will also strengthen your ability to use self-hypnosis as a lifelong tool for change.

Daily Routine 26 & 27

1. Do the Heart to Yes technique.
2. Practice mindfulness meditation for ten minutes.
3. Journal for five to ten minutes.
4. Find a skill you want to improve or a behavior you want to change and use the Ego State technique while in a trance. To apply the Ego State work on yourself, use the second variation of self-hypnosis and follow these four simple steps:

Step 1: Pre-Hypnosis—Set Your Intention

Before you do the hypnosis induction, decide exactly what you want to work on in trance.

- Be specific. Instead of "I want to be smarter," say "I want my unconscious mind to help me learn

more effectively and faster and apply what I learn with ease. Together, we will use the Ego State work to accomplish this goal."
- Remember: state it in **positive terms**: focus on what you *do* want, not what you don't want.
- Decide how long you'll stay in trance (for example, twenty minutes).
- Decide how you want to feel afterward: refreshed and energized, or relaxed and ready for sleep.

Step 2: Induction—Entering Trance

Use the *Breathing With the Eyes* or the induction of your choice.

- Sit or lie down in a safe and quiet space, ensure you won't get distracted. If you tend to fall asleep, choose a sitting position.
- Pick a point across the room to focus on.
- As you inhale deeply, open your eyes wide (exaggerate the movement) as if you're breathing in through them.
- As you exhale, close your eyes slowly, imagining your eyelids are heavy and relaxed.
- Repeat this three to five times, each time letting your eyelids feel heavier.
- On the final exhale, keep your eyes closed.

Step 3: Deepening the Trance—Going Further In

Deepening makes the trance more conducive to change.

- Imagine a staircase in front of you.

- With each step down, count backward from ten to one, feeling yourself going deeper into your unconscious mind.
- You might imagine it getting darker, quieter, or more peaceful as you descend. You can say to yourself "going deeper" with each step.
- Stop when you feel deeply relaxed and ready to work.

Step 4: The Work—You Lead the Session

Once you're in trance, invite your Higher Self or Inner Strength part to step forward and help guide the process. Ask if there are any parts involved in the behavior or skill you want to change or improve, and request permission to speak with them directly. One at a time, allow these parts to become executive so you can learn their name, age, and role. Listen without judgment as they share their perspective, and thank them for the ways they've tried to help you in the past. When it feels right, suggest new roles or strategies that better serve your current goals, always seeking their consent before making changes. If helpful, invite other parts to support the process, create alliances, or offer resources. Continue until all parts agree on the change, then thank them before emerging from trance.

Step 5: Coming Out of Hypnosis—Returning to Full Awareness

- You used the staircase to deepen the trance, imagine climbing back up, step by step, becoming more alert with each number.
- If you want to return from trance feeling awake and refreshed, when you open your eyes, stretch

or move gently before standing. Take a moment to notice how you feel.

Stay positive as you practice hypnosis. You won't master it overnight, but each session sharpens your skills. And soon, the process will get easier and eventually feel like second nature.

In the next chapter, we'll explore a tool that complements our self-hypnosis skills and helps enhance our daily lives: Visualization++.

8. Visualization++

You've probably heard of visualization before, maybe in the context of athletes mentally rehearsing their performance to improve their results. In this chapter, we're going to explore something I call Visualization++, which is based on similar principles but takes the concept much further. I chose the name partly because it's catchy, but also because this approach truly goes beyond standard visualization. Most people think of visualization as just creating pictures or mental movies, but when we engage other sensory systems, such as auditory (sound) and kinesthetic (feeling), along with the visual, the effect becomes dramatically more powerful. By using all three systems together, we can change the way we perceive the world, shift how we feel internally, and create deep, lasting transformations.

Visualization++ techniques can be used on their own, but they also work beautifully in a hypnotic trance, where the critical faculty is bypassed and suggestions go directly to the unconscious mind. Hypnosis acts like an amplifier, making the process even more powerful, but even without it, Visualization++ is highly effective. In fact, the way we'll be practicing here will already put you in a light trance, simply by centering your awareness behind your eyes, focusing in the middle of your head, and taking a few deep breaths, you'll naturally begin shifting into a trance.

Before we jump into the first technique, let's look more closely at the three sensory systems we'll be using. The visual system is the most familiar for most people. This is how we create images and moving pictures (movies) in our minds. These images can be large or small, vivid and colorful or dim and grainy. We can imagine ourselves inside the image, experiencing it directly, or watching it from a distance, as if on a screen. We can speed up a movie, slow it down, or even freeze it, and all of these adjustments can dramatically change how we experience the memory or imagined scene.

The auditory system involves everything we hear. We can adjust the volume, pitch, or tempo of a sound, or even remove sound entirely. We can add new sounds, like background music or sound effects, to change the emotional tone of what we're experiencing. For example, adding circus music to an anxious memory can suddenly make it seem playful and far less intimidating.

Finally, the kinesthetic system relates to physical sensations and feelings, both external and internal. This includes emotions, textures, temperature, weight, and movement. We can notice how our body feels in a particular memory or imagined scene and change those sensations, for example by making something warmer, lighter, softer, or more expansive. Many people overlook the kinesthetic element when they visualize, but incorporating it makes the experience far richer and more impactful.

When you combine all three systems: visual, auditory, and kinesthetic, you have a method that's far more powerful than using visuals alone. This is the heart of Visualization++, and in the next sections, you'll see just how quickly and effectively these adjustments can shift your perspective and your emotional state.

Let's dive into our first Visualization++ technique. It is simple, versatile, and surprisingly powerful: the Dimmer Switch.

Dimmer switch

This first Visualization++ technique is one of my personal favorites. I call it the Dimmer Switch, and there are so many reasons I love it.

For one thing, it gets us out of black-and-white, all-or-nothing thinking. Instead of on or off, good or bad, we start thinking in a more flexible, nuanced way, just like adjusting the brightness in a room. My background is in computer science, and I was trained to think in a deterministic way. Plus, I grew up thinking in binary terms: zero or one, yes or no, either/or. This behavior came from my personality, my education, and the way I was raised. This simple technique opened me up to more analog thinking, and that shift alone made me more adaptable in life.

The other reason I love it is because it's incredibly versatile. You can use it to calm your mind before meditation, wind down before bed, raise your energy in the morning, adjust your focus before a meeting, pretty much anything you want to dial up or down. Personally, I use it almost every time I meditate to quiet my mind before I begin.

Here's how it works:

Imagine that right in the center of your head, you create a dimmer switch. It can be a dial, a slider, or whatever control feels natural to you. Then, you give it a clear meaning. For example, if you're using it for meditation, one end of the scale could mean "no thinking at all," and the other end could mean "my mind is racing with chatter."

Now, the fun part: you **turn down or up** whatever you want to **reduce or increase**. I often use my dimmer switch to quiet my thinking, and I add visual and sensory elements to make it more powerful. For example, as I turn the dial toward zero, the space in my head gets darker and quieter, as if the lights are fading out and the noise is disappearing. You could also imagine hearing chatter that gradually fades away, or music that slows down and softens until it's silent.

The beauty of this technique is that you can customize it endlessly. You can add color, maybe your "busy mind" setting glows red and gradually shifts to a calming blue as you turn it down. You could add temperature and sensation, maybe it feels warm and restless when set to "high" and cool and soothing as you lower it. The only rule is to keep it simple enough to use quickly when you need it.

And remember, you can also use it to turn things up. Let's say you wake up in the morning feeling sluggish. You could have your Dimmer Switch control your energy level, with one end representing complete lethargy, while the other glows with lively, buzzing energy. All you need to do is picture yourself sliding or turning the control toward the energy you want and notice how it begins to build within you.

I've used it before bed too. If my mind is buzzing, I imagine my "thinking" slider going down slowly until it's silent, and then I drift into sleep. Sometimes I combine it with a gentle self-hypnosis trance, which makes it even more effective.

How to Try It Yourself

Start by sitting, standing, or lying down comfortably. Close your eyes if you want, it can help, but it's not necessary. Bring your awareness behind your eyes and take a few deep breaths. Then, move that awareness to the center of your head. This is where you'll imagine your dimmer switch.

Design it in your mind. Is it a big, chunky dial you can grab and turn? A sleek slider? Maybe a futuristic control panel with a single glowing lever? Once you see it, decide exactly what it controls: your thinking, your energy, your focus, your calmness, whatever you want. Set one end of the scale to "low" and the other to "high," and make those extremes vivid.

Now, physically reach out with your hand and move the control. You can also do it entirely in your mind, but adding a kinesthetic movement, actually grabbing the dial or sliding the control, makes it even more real and powerful. As you adjust it, notice what changes in your body and mind. Add visuals, sounds, and sensations that match the change. If you're turning down chatter, maybe the space in your head gets darker, the sound fades away, and your muscles relax. If you're turning up energy, maybe colors brighten, the air feels fresher, and a lively soundtrack starts playing in the background.

You can also aim for a balance point instead of an extreme. For example, if you tend to be either over-energized or completely drained, you could use your dimmer to find that "just right" middle setting. The goal is to find the level that serves you in the moment and learn to adjust it as easily as you'd adjust the lights in a room.

The more you play with this, the more natural it becomes. Over time, you'll be able to just think of your dimmer switch and instantly adjust your internal state.

As you move through your day, keep your routine alive. Start with the Heart to Yes technique to connect with your intentions, follow it with a few minutes of mindfulness meditation, and give yourself the gift of journaling to process your thoughts and feelings. Then, for today's practice, play with the Dimmer Switch Visualization++ technique. Choose a real situation in your life where you'd like to turn something up or down, this could be sharpening your focus before meditation, getting drowsy before bed, or boosting your gratitude in the morning. Approach it with curiosity, make it your own, and enjoy the subtle but powerful shift it creates.

This simple but flexible technique is one you can return to anytime you want to shift your internal state. Let's put it into practice.

Daily Routine 28

1. Do the Heart to Yes technique.
2. Practice mindfulness meditation for ten minutes.
3. Journal for five to ten minutes.
4. Practice the *Dimmer Switch* Visualization++ technique. Choose a context where you want to either boost something (like your ability to memorize before studying) or reduce it (like the anxiety you might experience before going on a date).

Dress for Success

This next one is a lot of fun, and I call it Dress for Success. If you've studied Neuro-Linguistic Programming (NLP), you might have seen something similar called the Circle of Excellence. In my version, I love that it gets your body moving a little more. You're not just imagining a garment, you're physically stepping into it, as if you're putting on an outfit.

What's great about this approach is that it engages all the sensory systems: seeing the outfit, feeling it against your skin, even hearing a soundtrack that enhances the mood and adding movements to elevate the experience which makes it easier to re-enter the powerful state you're creating.

And that's what this technique is all about: stepping into an empowering state on purpose. Maybe it's confidence before a presentation, focus for an important meeting, calmness for a difficult conversation, or playful romance before a date. Whatever the situation, you create an outfit in your mind that represents the state you need, and then you put it on. When you wear it, you feel it. And later, you can use a small movement, like adjusting the collar, smoothing the cuffs, tipping a hat, to bring that state back instantly.

Let's say you're giving a presentation and want to feel powerful, confident, and inspiring. You might imagine a sharp black power suit, perfectly tailored to you. Maybe the fabric feels smooth and strong, the lines clean and perfect. Or perhaps you want to feel more light and flow, in this case you imagine a suit made entirely of shimmering light that glows with your own confidence and presence.

And here's the fun part: your outfit can be anything. It can be formal or casual, serious or silly, grounded or magical. You can add a hat, boots, a flowing cape, a bright scarf, anything that adds to the feeling you want. It can even include imaginary elements like glowing colors, swirling energy, or your favorite song playing when you put it on.

For example, I once imagined a date night outfit that made me feel romantic, confident, and witty. I pictured a black suit with a pink handkerchief in the pocket and a playful curly-haired wig. And the soundtrack? Let's Get It On by Marvin Gaye, of course. That combination made me feel charming and funny, exactly the state I wanted.

This works just as well for other states. Maybe you want to embody a calm authority before a tough meeting; your outfit might be a soft grey suit that feels warm and steady. Or maybe you want a burst of joy and playfulness, and so you create something bright and colorful that practically bounces with energy.

How to Do It Step-by-Step

Stand up if you can. Optionally close your eyes, it often helps with visualization. Bring your awareness behind your eyes, take a few deep breaths, and then move that awareness to the center of your head. Breathe deeply again, feeling your body standing tall and strong.

Now imagine the outfit in front of you. Build it piece by piece. What color is it? What's it made of? How does it feel to touch? Does it have a scent, a sound, or a kind of energy swirling around it? Make it as vivid and specific as you can.

When you're ready, physically step into the outfit. Put on the jacket, adjust the cuffs, slip on the shoes, fasten the buttons, or place the hat on your head. As you do this, feel yourself stepping into the state you've chosen. Now amplify it! Recall times in your life when you've felt that way before, or imagine how someone you admire would feel in that state. Make it bigger, stronger, more real.

When the feeling is at its peak, choose one small, specific movement to anchor it. It could be straightening your tie, tipping your hat, smoothing your skirt, flicking your collar, any small and repeatable movement. And if you want, pair it with a word or sound that makes you smile or feel powerful. For me, it's "Yes!" because I've anchored that word to pride, joy, and self-belief through the Heart to Yes technique. But you can choose anything, a "Yeah!", a "Boom!", or even an animal sound if it makes you grin.

Anchoring is a way to attach a specific state to a small trigger, like a touch, a gesture, or a word, so you can bring that feeling back whenever you need it. Think of it like creating a shortcut in your nervous system. You practice the state (thoughts, feelings and physiology) you want and pair it with a consistent action.

Once anchored, you can use this movement and your chosen word to instantly bring back that state anytime you need it. And just like any favorite outfit, it works best if you take care of it. To do this, I suggest you reapply the state now and then by revisiting the Dress for Success technique, strengthening the feelings, and keeping it fresh.

One more tip: sometimes the best states to anchor happen naturally, without planning. For example, recently I was at an ecstatic dance event. I was moving freely, full of joy and energy, and also felt this deep sense of calm. I felt like everything was going to be okay. Out of nowhere, I decided to capture that feeling. In my mind, I put on a bright white tuxedo with a top hat, and I anchored it with the simple movement of tipping the hat. Now, whenever I do that movement, I can bring back the joy and calm I felt that night in seconds.

The possibilities here are endless. The key is to play, experiment, and have fun with it. The more you make it your own, the more powerful it becomes.

For today's daily routine, I invite you to make this practice your own and bring out your imagination for the Dress for Success exercise. Choose a state you want to embody today—confidence, joy, calm, romance, focus, anything—and design your outfit down to the smallest detail. Put it on in your mind, adjust it, step fully into that state, and anchor it with your chosen movement and word. Carry it with you for the rest of the day, ready to slip it on anytime you need that boost.

This practice blends imagination with embodiment, letting you step into your best self at will. Let's capture it in today's routine.

Daily Routine 29

1. Do the Heart to Yes technique.
2. Practice mindfulness meditation for ten minutes.
3. Journal for five to ten minutes.
4. Practice the Dress for Success technique. Design an outfit for the state you want to embody. For example: being confident, being an effective communicator, being in a joyful mood. Amplify the state using all the sensory systems and their properties. Put on the outfit. Act it out physically.

The Transmuting Shape

This is the last Visualization++ technique we'll explore together, and honestly, it's my favorite. I love it because it's incredibly versatile and can be applied in so many situations, whether it's reframing the past, calming anxiety about the future, or shifting how we feel about ourselves right now. It's especially useful for dealing with memories that haunt us, emotions that feel overwhelming, or worries that keep us stuck. And the best part? It works fast.

At its core, the Transmuting Shape is about taking a problem, anything from a difficult memory to a heavy feeling or future anxiety, and turning it into something we can see, feel, and even hear. Then, by using the visual, auditory, and kinesthetic systems we've talked about, we change its properties in ways that transform how we experience it. Sometimes that means shrinking it, moving it, smoothing it out, or even exploding it into positive energy. Other times, it means keeping it, but altering it so it feels safe, peaceful, and manageable.

Here's how to do it. We start the way we usually do, taking a few deep breaths, closing our eyes, and getting comfortable sitting or lying down. Put your awareness behind your eyes, and then slowly move it into the center of your head. Breathe deeply here for a few moments. When you're ready, bring to mind the problem you want to work with. Notice where it is in relation to you. Is it inside your body, on your skin, or floating somewhere outside you? Now begin to imagine it as a shape. It could be two-dimensional or three-dimensional. It might have a single color, multiple colors, or no color at all. Maybe it's spiky, smooth, rough, soft, hollow, solid, heavy, or light. Does it make a sound? A sad song, a loud hum, a steady pulse? Or is it silent?

Once you've defined the shape in as much detail as possible, start changing it in ways that make you feel better. You might push it far away until it's just a dot in the distance, then let it dissolve into light and release its energy back into the universe. You might change its texture from sharp to smooth, or its color from dark to bright. You might shrink it down to something tiny and harmless, or move it to a different location in or around your body that feels better.

I once worked with a client who had a very uncomfortable feeling sitting right in their chest. They described it as a spiky black ball that made it hard to breathe. I asked if they wanted to get rid of it completely, but they said no, they wanted to keep it, and just change it. So we explored what would make it more bearable. In the end, they made it smooth, turned it into a peaceful sky-blue, and imagined it filled with calm water. It also made a soft, soothing sound. Then they moved it behind their back, where it felt less intrusive. When they opened their eyes, their whole posture had changed. They looked lighter, calmer. Weeks later, they told me they still felt the benefits of that shift.

This technique isn't just for removing discomfort, it can also be used to enhance positive states. For example, if you want to remain calm in stressful situations, you can create a shape that represents calm for you. Maybe it's a cool, pale-green sphere that hums gently and feels soft and warm in your hands. You can place it inside your chest, around your body like a bubble, or anywhere that makes it easy to access when you need it. You can even physically mime moving it into place, which adds the kinesthetic dimension and makes the change more powerful.

The Transmuting Shape works because it gives your unconscious mind a clear, sensory-rich way to reshape your experience. You're not just thinking positively, you're rewiring how your brain processes that memory, feeling, or fear. Every time you do it, you're creating new neural pathways that make it easier to respond in more useful, empowering ways.

It's important to note that each person represents problem states differently and the shapes they choose and how they transform them vary greatly. Some might find the color blue and a soft lullaby soothing, while others might find them irritating. The practice of the Transmuting Shape and most of the other techniques we have explored in this book is highly personal; we can encourage each other but avoid comparisons. *We must practice for our own wellbeing and personal growth with compassion and self-love.*

Today, I invite you to choose one thing you'd like to transform: a troubling memory, a heavy feeling, an anxious thought, or a state you want to strengthen. Close your eyes, find a shape for it, and then start playing. Change its size, texture, color, sound, and location until it feels right. Really allow yourself to experiment. The more vividly you engage your senses, the more powerful the shift will be. When you've shaped it into something that serves you, anchor that feeling by taking a deep breath and fully experiencing your new state. Then, carry it with you into the rest of your life.

Daily Routine 30

1. Do the Heart to Yes technique.
2. Practice mindfulness meditation for ten minutes.
3. Journal for five to ten minutes.
4. Practice the Transmuting Shape technique. Think of a problem, represent it as a shape. To do so, use all systems: visual, auditory and kinesthetic. And transmute the shape until you feel empowered.

Here are a few tips for your Transmuting Shape practice:

- You can assess the problem before you start on a scale from zero to ten, where zero is no stress at all and ten is pulling your hair out. Try to make it as high as you can.
- Shake it out.
- Then do the Transmuting Shape technique
    - **Get comfortable**: Sit or lie down, close your eyes, and take a few deep breaths.
    - **Shift your awareness**: Place it behind your eyes, then move it into the center of your head. Take a few more deep breaths.

- **Create the shape**: Imagine it as a physical object:
    - Where is it (inside, outside, around you)?
    - What shape is it (2D or 3D)?
    - What color(s) does it have?
    - What texture or surface qualities does it have?
    - Is it heavy or light, still or moving?
    - Does it make a sound or is it silent?
- **Alter the properties**: Adjust size, color, texture, movement, or sound until it feels better.
- **Change its position**: Move it closer, further, inside you, outside you, wherever it feels most useful.
- **Decide its fate**: Keep it in its new form, transform it further, or dissolve/release it completely.
- **Anchor the change**: Take a deep breath, fully experience the new state, and notice how it feels in your body.
- **Return to the present**: Wiggle your fingers and toes, then open your eyes, bringing the transformed feeling with you.

- And after the technique, check again. How does it feel now? Did the number you picked at the beginning lowered?
- You can repeat the technique if needed. Most of the time, once will suffice.

The Dimmer Switch, Dress for Success and Transmuting Shape are meant to be personal and adaptable. Use it in the way that best serves you.

When Should You Use Visualization++?

I encourage you to use the Visualization++ techniques often. If you want to practice self-hypnosis, it's a great idea to put yourself in a trance and then use one of these techniques. The trance acts as an amplifier, allowing the changes you create to sink in more deeply.

You can also combine what you've learned here with other tools in this book, particularly Timeline and Ego State work. For example, when working with ego states, you can change their clothing, the way they feel, or even how they see the world. Working with your timeline, when you want to brighten your future, you can literally tweak elements you see on your timeline, making them more vivid, more colorful, and more powerful until you naturally step into the state you desire.

By now, you know how to turn down unwanted and turn up desirable experiences with the Dimmer Switch, whether that's quieting mental chatter or dialing up your energy when you need it. You've learned how to create a powerful state and set a trigger for it, like in Dress for Success, where simply adjusting a cuff, tipping a hat, or saying your chosen word can instantly bring you into that state. You've also explored how to transform a challenging state using the Transmuting Shape, reshaping and redefining it until you relate to it differently, creating a more resourceful, useful frame of mind.

Now, with Visualization++ under your belt, on top of mindfulness, journaling, somatic techniques, and self-hypnosis, you have an incredibly rich toolkit for transformation. **The aim is not to create a life with no problems, but to build**

resilience and strength so that when difficulties arise, you can meet them from a place of inner power and calm. Remember that these techniques, as said for self-hypnosis, are not magic pills. For example, the Dimmer Switch will give you a boost of energy but if you are sleep deprived, I invite you to listen to your body and take the rest you need. It is also true for gaining confidence, the techniques shown in this book will help you, but you need to put time and effort into building skills that will support the confidence you seek.

These tools aren't just techniques, they're practices, and practices only work when you use them consistently. I know it can be tempting to skip your daily routine when life gets busy, but *you deserve the benefits that come from consistency. Over time, these habits will shape the way you think, feel, and act.*

I believe in you, and I hope that by now your belief in yourself has grown as well. You truly have everything you need right now to create meaningful changes. In the chapters ahead, we'll explore how to set healthy boundaries, how to choose and strengthen beliefs that serve you, and how to further discover who you truly are. These next steps will bring together all the tools you've learned so far, showing you how to apply them in new, powerful ways.

And remember, you're not alone in this journey. Our community group is there for you. Join our community at https://members.jftiger.com. Use it to connect, share your wins and challenges, ask questions, and learn from the experiences of others. I'll be there too, answering questions and cheering you on.

For now, have fun with these techniques. Play with them. Personalize them. Make them part of your life. The more you use them, the more they'll shape your mind, your state, and your future.

Today, you'll bring it all together. Start with the **Heart to Yes** technique to connect with your inner strength, then give yourself ten minutes of **mindfulness meditation** to settle your mind. Spend five to ten minutes **journaling** to capture your thoughts, feelings, and insights. Once you're centered, choose one of the **Visualization++** techniques, whether it's the Dimmer Switch, Dress for Success, or the Transmuting Shape, and practice it while in a trance to deepen its impact. Finish by doing a **somatic technique** of your choice to reconnect with your body and release any remaining tension. This is your chance to use your full toolkit in one flow, building the habits and resilience that will carry you forward.

Daily Routine 31

1. Do the Heart to Yes technique.
2. Practice mindfulness meditation for ten minutes.
3. Journal for five to ten minutes.
4. Practice one of the Visualization++ techniques while in a trance.
5. Practice a somatic technique of your choice.

In the next chapter, we'll explore how setting healthy boundaries supports everything you've learned so far, giving you the structure to protect your growth and live authentically.

9. Setting Healthy Boundaries

Boundaries are the limits and expectations we set for ourselves and for others, and they exist to protect what matters most to us: our values. They can take many forms: physical, sexual, emotional, spiritual, or boundaries around our time and energy. In fact, by committing to your daily routine throughout this journey, you've already set a boundary for yourself. That's a form of self-boundary, an agreement with yourself about how you will show up.

When we set boundaries for others, it might sound like: "If you cheat on me, I'm leaving you," or "If you keep yelling at me right now, I'm going to step away, and we can discuss this later." These examples are clear and direct, but boundaries don't always have to be rigid or all-or-nothing. They can have nuances, and sometimes it's necessary to talk through those nuances, either with ourselves or with others, to create a version of the boundary that truly works.

For example, one of my weekend boundaries for my children is that they go to bed at 10:30 p.m. That means their bedtime routine is done, and they're tucked into bed, ready to sleep. If they want to stay up later, they have until supper time to ask permission. We'll discuss it, and I'll give them my decision by then. It's a flexible boundary but still very clear. And because it's clear, it's easier for them and for me to follow.

I see boundaries as contracts. A well-written contract is easy to follow; a vague one isn't very useful. It can have flexibility, but the clearer it is, the more likely it is to be respected, by us and by the people around us.

Now that we've defined what boundaries are and how they can look in real life, let's explore why they're essential and what happens when they're missing.

Why Do You Need Boundaries?

Do I handle boundaries well? I'm getting better, but if I'm being honest, I still have a long way to go. For a long time, my inability to set proper boundaries led me straight into burnout and more than once, unfortunately. I would let my work spill over into my personal time, giving away my evenings, weekends, and even my mental space to work. In my personal life, I wasn't much better. Resentment built up in my romantic relationship because I failed to set clear boundaries, not just for my ex, but for myself too. I didn't protect my time, my needs, or my energy, and over time, that made everything much more difficult.

I believe that most people struggle to set and maintain healthy boundaries. I don't need a study to prove it, I just have to look around. I see people who are constantly exhausted, stressed, frustrated, and running on fumes. Many neglect themselves, not out of laziness or lack of willpower, but because they allow others, or themselves, to repeatedly cross their boundaries.

Here's the truth: every surge of frustration, irritation, or anger often signals a boundary has been crossed. We've already spent a lot of time in this book learning how to deal with difficult emotions and challenging thoughts. But wouldn't it be even better to reduce the number of times we're put into those situations in the first place? That's what healthy boundaries can do. They won't protect us from every challenge, life is still going to throw curveballs at us, but they can significantly reduce the emotional drain caused by avoidable situations.

Sometimes, the first step to setting healthy boundaries is simply recognizing that we need one. There are signs, subtle at first, that start to tell us something's off. We might notice a growing resentment toward a person, a situation, or even toward ourselves. Maybe we feel drained every time we interact with someone, or we catch ourselves avoiding them altogether. Perhaps we're saying yes when we desperately want to say no, and afterward, we feel frustrated or even angry at ourselves.

Another sign is when we're constantly overextended, too many commitments, too little time or energy for our own needs. If you find yourself compromising your values just to keep the peace or to avoid disappointing someone, **that's a red flag**. And here's one more: if you often replay conversations in your head, wishing you had spoken up, it's likely a sign that your boundaries were crossed and your voice went unheard.

Pay attention to these signals. They're not just inconveniences, they're your mind and body letting you know it's time to take action, to protect your time, your energy, and your well-being.

When we set clear boundaries, we set clear expectations. And when we follow through on them consistently, we protect our energy, preserve our well-being, and drastically reduce the resentment and frustration that can poison our relationships with others and with ourselves.

For today, I invite you to take what we've just covered and explore it in your daily routine. Spend some time reflecting on the areas of your life where you might need boundaries, whether those boundaries are with yourself or with others. Write them down, and note who they are for. If you want to go deeper, use the Punching and Kicking somatic technique to help you connect physically to your sense of boundaries. Sometimes engaging the body makes the emotional and mental aspects much clearer.

With this awareness in mind, let's turn it into practice by reflecting on the areas of life where boundaries are needed most.

Daily Routine 32

1. Do the Heart to Yes technique.
2. Practice mindfulness meditation for ten minutes.
3. Journal for five to ten minutes.
4. Spend some time listing areas of your life where you think you need boundaries. Write down what they are and who they are for. Here's a Tip:
   - Use the Punching and Kicking somatic technique to help you explore your boundaries.

How To Set Healthy Boundaries

Let's talk about how to set healthy and clear boundaries. I won't sugarcoat it: this can be challenging. But it's absolutely possible, and the best place to start is with ourselves. That's why, throughout this book, I've encouraged you to make contracts with yourself and follow through. Every time you kept your commitment to complete the daily routine, you were already practicing setting and maintaining boundaries.

When you're getting started, focus on small, quick wins. This creates momentum, makes the process less overwhelming and builds trust. For example, if you sometimes struggle to get out of bed in the morning, set a boundary with yourself: within five minutes of my alarm going off, I'll be in the shower. Then honor that commitment every single time. That consistency is the foundation of every strong boundary and *it's how you begin to trust yourself to follow through.*

The same principle applies to boundaries with other people, clarity and follow-through are key. If you say "If you keep yelling, I'm leaving," and the yelling continues, you don't wait, you leave. Not as a punishment or threat, but as an act of self-respect. I'll be honest, when I first started setting boundaries with people, I felt like the bad guy. I felt guilty. But over time, I realized those feelings were simply the discomfort of breaking old patterns. What allowed me to stand firm was the self-love and self-compassion I'd been building through the very techniques I've shared with you in this book.

When you set boundaries, remember: they're not about punishing people, they exist to protect your well-being. And when it comes to consequences, whether for yourself or others, make sure they're realistic. For instance, if I told myself, "If I skip the gym today, I won't have dessert". And I know I might still have dessert anyway, that wouldn't be an effective consequence for me. Only set boundaries and consequences you know you can uphold. Otherwise, the boundary loses its meaning and power.

Clear. Consistent. Follow-through. Those three elements will make your boundaries strong and sustainable. Once we begin practicing setting boundaries for ourselves, we're ready to strengthen boundaries with others, and that's where resistance often shows up.

Expect Pushbacks

When I first began setting boundaries with my romantic partner, it was not smooth sailing. I faced pushbacks, and it was uncomfortable. That discomfort is completely normal. Whenever you introduce new boundaries, expect resistance. People are adjusting to a new dynamic, and you're adjusting too. That's why it's your responsibility to be clear about your boundaries, to communicate them, and to consistently follow through with consequences when boundaries are crossed.

Some boundaries leave room for discussion and flexibility, and it's important to explore those nuances. Let's look at two examples. The first is a self-boundary. Imagine someone who highly values their health and wants to train at the gym every day. But they also deeply value spending time with their family. On especially busy days, they might adapt their boundaries, doing a shorter workout at home instead of going to the gym, so they can still honor both values. The boundary is upheld, but in a way that's realistic and balanced.

The second example comes from a story I heard from Simon Sinek, which I love because it shows how boundaries with others can still be flexible. During a meeting, an employee tells their boss, "I'm happy to work my assigned hours, but I don't want to do overtime. I need that time for my family." The boss replies, "I respect that, but there may be rare occasions, once every month or two months, when I need you to work overtime or even on a weekend. If that happens, I'll make sure you get a full day off afterward." The employee agrees, knowing that if overtime starts happening more than once a month, the agreement will need to be revisited. This is a perfect example of boundaries that are both clear and adaptable.

Whether you're dealing with self-boundaries or boundaries with others, the keys remain the same: clearly state your limit, follow through with the agreed-upon consequences, and stay consistent. And remember, setting healthy boundaries isn't about being harsh or uncaring. It's an act of self-respect, one that builds your sense of self-worth. When pushbacks come, you can use meditation or self-hypnosis to stay grounded, patient, and compassionate, both toward yourself and toward others, while still holding the line.

When you're communicating your boundary to someone, it helps to have language that's simple, clear, and firm without being aggressive. Here are some sample phrases you can adapt to your own situation:

- "I'm not available for that."
- "I can't talk about this right now. Let's revisit it later."
- "If you continue yelling, I will leave the room."
- "I'm not comfortable with that. Please stop."
- "I need some time to myself right now."
- "I understand that's important to you, but I need to take care of myself first."
- "No, thank you." (You don't owe anyone more explanation if you don't want to give one).
- "I can do this, but not that."
- "I won't be able to help if it means working past my set hours."
- "If this happens again, here's what I will do…"

These phrases give you a starting point. Adjust them so they sound like you, and remember: the power is in your clarity, your follow-through, and your tone. Calm, steady, and certain.

For today's daily routine, I invite you to choose one or two of the self-boundaries you identified yesterday and turn them into clear contracts with yourself. Commit to honoring these boundaries consistently, and be ready to follow through on the consequences you've set. To make it easier, use self-hypnosis to tap into your inner resources, strengthen your resolve, and reinforce your belief in your ability to stick to your commitments. Think of this as a way to train both your mind and your habits, gradually building trust with yourself one choice at a time.

Now, let's practice turning yesterday's reflections into clear self-contracts, building confidence and consistency in small steps.

Daily Routine 33

1. Do the Heart to Yes technique.
2. Practice mindfulness meditation for ten minutes.
3. Journal for five to ten minutes.
4. Choose one or two self-boundaries you wrote about yesterday and put them in place and commit to the contract. Use self-hypnosis to help you find the resources you need to stick with those boundaries.

Putting It All Together

In today's daily routine, I invite you to set at least one healthy boundary with someone else. Before you do, take a moment to focus on being gentle with yourself and with the other person. To help you enter the right state of mind, you can start with a loving-kindness meditation, directing compassion toward both yourself and them. You might also use self-hypnosis to draw on inner resources for staying compassionate, speaking clearly, and communicating effectively. The clearer your contract is, the easier it will be for everyone involved to understand and respect.

Don't be afraid to allow for flexibility where it feels appropriate, but remember: you deserve to set and uphold healthy boundaries. This is a powerful act of self-care. Somatic techniques can also help you discover where new boundaries might be needed. For instance, using the Punching and Kicking exercise, and repeating "No, no," can uncover emotions and memories that point to areas where limits are necessary.

You can also use simple but profound techniques to generate compassion, such as placing your hand over your heart for at least twenty seconds. This small act can bring a deep sense of calm, self-love, and empathy toward yourself and the other person. Doing this before a boundary conversation can help you feel grounded, centered, and confident in your message.

Be brave, be clear, and be consistent. You deserve to protect your time, body, energy, and emotional well-being. Setting boundaries is not selfish, it's an essential part of honoring your worth and caring for yourself. I believe in you.

If you'd like to explore this topic in greater depth, I highly recommend the book Set Boundaries, Find Peace by

Nedra Glover Tawwab. It's a wonderful resource that can give you even more tools and perspectives for creating healthy, sustainable boundaries in every area of your life.

Daily Routine 34

1. Do the Heart to Yes technique.
2. Practice mindfulness meditation for ten minutes.
3. Journal for five to ten minutes.
4. I invite you to set at least one boundary with one person and communicate that boundary with them. Here are some ideas to help you:
   - Remember to be clear, communicate with gentleness and stick to what you say.
   - To help you, you can do a loving-kindness meditation before you communicate your boundaries.
   - I also suggest you do self-hypnosis to help you find the resources you need to communicate effectively and gently, and find the courage to stick to what you say.

As we move forward, these boundaries will serve as a foundation for the next layer of growth: adopting beliefs that empower and support the life you're building.

10. Adopting Useful Beliefs

Believing is the feeling that something or someone exists, is true, or is trustworthy.

I used to think beliefs were forever. I believed that once you believed something, it was set in stone. I also believed that for me to truly believe in something, it had to be absolutely true. For example, I once believed in one God, and in my mind, that belief was unquestionably right. If someone didn't believe in God—or didn't believe in the same God as me—then they were automatically wrong. I was rigid in my thinking and had no room for other perspectives.

But over time, life proved me wrong. My experiences taught me that beliefs can change, *and that it's far more helpful, may I say useful,* **to see beliefs not as true or false, but as useful or not useful.** That shift in thinking has given me far more compassion and understanding for other people's beliefs, even when they're very different from mine.

Let me illustrate this point with a story. Imagine someone is lost in the forest, let's call him Jim. He believes that people are out there searching for him right now. In reality, that might not be true, no one might even know he is missing yet. But the belief keeps him calm. It keeps Jim focused on finding shelter, staying warm, and keeping himself safe through the night. Even if it's not factually true, it's useful.

That's what I believe about beliefs now, and I invite you to adopt the same mindset. If a belief empowers you to reach your goals, fulfill your needs, or keep going when things are hard, it's useful. If a belief holds you back, discourages you, or makes you doubt your worth, it's not useful: it's a limiting belief.

A limiting belief is like a weight tied to our ankle while we're trying to swim. A useful belief is like a life vest, helping us stay afloat and move forward.

In today's routine, I invite you to take a deep, honest look at the beliefs you carry with you. Grab your journal and make two lists: one of the useful, empowering beliefs that help you grow and move forward, and one of the limiting beliefs that no longer serve you. As you write, ask yourself: Where did each belief come from? Was it born out of your own life experience, or was it planted by someone else's words and ideas? This exercise is not about judging yourself, it's about gaining clarity. Once you see your beliefs laid out in front of you, you can start choosing which ones to keep and which ones to let go.

Daily Routine 35

1. Do the Heart to Yes technique.
2. Practice mindfulness meditation for ten minutes.
3. Journal for five to ten minutes.
4. Make two lists: one for the empowering beliefs that support you, and one for the limiting beliefs that no longer serve you. Reflect on where they come from: your own experience or the words of others.

Changing Your Beliefs

How do we remove limiting beliefs and install useful ones? First, let's look at removing the limiting ones. Take the list you made of beliefs that hold you back and go through them one by one. Your goal is to challenge each belief and look for evidence that it isn't absolutely true. This is where curiosity becomes your best friend. Read books, search online, and listen to subject matter experts. Ask people you respect for their perspective. You're looking for cracks in the wall, proof that there's another way to see things. Look for as many perspectives as you can to expand your understanding of the belief. Be courageous and seek out perspectives you might have avoided before, simply because you feared they would change your mind.

Let me give you a specific example. Imagine you've been reading this book but find yourself resisting self-hypnosis because you believe it isn't real, or that it's not based on science. If you hold that belief, it's going to be very difficult to use some of the techniques I showed you. So what can you do? You start by researching. Look for studies showing the effectiveness of hypnosis. You might find neuroscience articles explaining how the brain responds in trance, or read about hospitals using it for pain management and anxiety reduction. Then, go one step further: talk to people who have actually benefited from it. Ask them how it worked for them.

For me personally, I've met countless people in my hypnosis training who have built powerful, fulfilling lives by using self-hypnosis consistently. You might even use one of the self-hypnosis techniques we explore to convince yourself it works. I was skeptical at first. I even had a limiting belief telling me that my disability would prevent me from entering a trance. Yet I found that wasn't true at all.

I'm still uncovering limiting beliefs. I don't know how many times I postponed writing this book because I had a limiting belief about my writing skills or the value I can bring to people through it. But I used the very techniques I've shared with you and surrounded myself with friends who believed in me. And look at me now. *I believe you can break free of your limiting beliefs too.*

Once you've started to weaken an unhelpful belief, the next step is to replace it with an empowering one. Think about your goals, desires, and needs. What beliefs would make it easier for you to achieve them? Maybe you want to feel more confident in your ability to adapt to change. A useful belief might be: I can handle whatever comes my way. You already have some empowering beliefs on your list, and you can create new ones.

One of my own most useful beliefs came from my days as a senior developer. I adopted the mindset that every problem had at least one solution, and that with effort and persistence, I could figure anything out. That belief became a kind of superpower for me. I remember leading a project where one of my team members, a talented but less-experienced developer, would sometimes spend hours wrestling with a tricky bug. When they finally called me over, I would often solve it in under ten minutes (I'll admit, I was a bit of a show-off back then, and probably still am). But what stood out wasn't my speed or skills, it was the belief gap between us. They were convinced the software component we were using was flawed and simply couldn't do what we needed it to do. That limiting belief alone shut down their creativity before they even tried. Over time, I watched them replace this belief with a far more empowering one, such as *I'm a really good developer* and *I can figure out very complex problems*. And when that shift happened, their ability to solve problems exploded.

Once you've chosen a belief, use the tools you've been learning to install it. This is where self-hypnosis really shines. Put yourself into a trance and use the Transmuting Shape. Imagine that belief as a shape, maybe it's a glowing sphere, smooth and warm, resting right in the center of your chest. You can give it a color, a texture, even a sound. Move it around in your body until it feels just right. When it's in the perfect place, take a deep breath and imagine it locking in, becoming part of you. Say to yourself, I believe this now.

Or use Ego State work. Imagine the part of you that already lives by this belief, and let it teach the rest of you how to feel and think this way. Journaling, somatic techniques, and meditation are also powerful ways to explore and reinforce your new belief. For example, in your journal, write your new belief ten times twice a day. Meditate on it. Use affirmations like "I am capable", "I am resourceful", "I am enough", or "I am a sex machine", and don't judge your beliefs ;-)

And don't underestimate the power of community. Being around people who live out your empowering belief can strengthen it in you. For me, my local dance community has been invaluable. They are open, nonjudgmental, and free-spirited, and just being around them reinforces my belief that I can grow, adapt, and live with joy. On the flip side, if you're surrounded by people who constantly reinforce a limiting belief, it's worth noticing how much that environment influences you. You don't necessarily have to cut ties, but awareness gives you choice.

Today, as part of your daily routine, I invite you to choose one new empowering belief and practice installing it using at least one of the techniques you've learned in this book. Find evidence for it, try it on "as if" it's already true, and notice how it feels. If it doesn't fit perfectly yet, that's okay, stay flexible and keep experimenting.

Daily Routine 36

1. Do the Heart to Yes technique.
2. Practice mindfulness meditation for ten minutes.
3. Journal for five to ten minutes.
4. Find a new belief that would be useful and empowering for you on your self-discovery journey and install it. Use some of the tools you learned in this book, consider using self-hypnosis and Visualization++, Dress for Success being an excellent choice here.

Let's build on the power of beliefs by exploring the values and layers of identity that shape our lives.

11. Adopting a Useful Identity

I believe our identity is shaped by our values, how well we know them, and how sincerely we live by them. And you'll soon discover how empowering adopting a useful identity can be.

Authenticity Is Key

Authenticity is one of those words we all love to nod along to, but living it day-to-day can be far trickier than it sounds. We're not just talking about being honest with others and ourselves, we're talking about showing up in a way that's real, even when it's uncomfortable or risky.

Imagine this: you're at a bar, hitting it off with someone new. You're having a great conversation, laughing, feeling that spark. Then, one of your favorite songs starts playing. You're excited—it's your song—and then they say, "Ugh, I hate this one." Now you have a choice. Do you smile and stay quiet so the vibe doesn't change? Or do you take a risk and say, "Actually, I love this song! I want to go dancing!" It sounds small, but that moment is a test of authenticity. And honestly, it's often harder than it seems to tell the truth about who we are and to show up authentically.

We even hide from ourselves. As I shared earlier in this book, for a long time I didn't want to face my feelings about my disability. I remember when I finally started eating my grand-maman's soup during the holidays, I was in my twenties. My grand-maman always made this incredibly delicious soup for New Year and every grandkid would sit on the stairs and eat together. But for me, eating soup was very difficult and uncomfortable, especially sitting on the stairs. I really wanted it, but I was sad and embarrassed by the way I looked while eating soup. Pretending those feelings didn't exist, and that I didn't want any, was my way of protecting myself, but it also meant I wasn't being fully authentic. No one would have judged me. I was blessed with a loving family. But it took me many years to fully show myself. And truthfully, I'm still working on it.

It helps to see authenticity not as an all-or-nothing concept, but as a spectrum. In some areas of life, we might live in full alignment with who we are, while in others, we hold back.

The point isn't to be perfect, it's to keep moving toward the real you.

The good news? Everything you've been practicing in this book, meditation, mindfulness, journaling, somatic techniques, self-hypnosis, Visualization++, have been building blocks for authenticity. Each one helps you notice your real thoughts and feelings, face them without flinching, and express them more openly.

So take a moment here. Think about how far you've come since the start of this journey. The courage needed to be honest with yourself. The progress you've made in understanding and accepting who you are. You deserve a pat on the back. You've done amazingly well! And in the next section, I'm going to share how I've been learning, and am still learning, to stay true to myself in a world that often rewards the opposite.

Identity and Values

One of the most powerful ways I've learned to understand myself is by exploring my core values. Your values are like your personal compass, they tell you what truly matters to you, even when life gets noisy and confusing.

I still remember being in university when one of my mentors asked me to make a list of my top core values. I froze. Not a single word came to mind. Looking back, I think there were two reasons for that. First, I was scared to really know who I was. Part of me didn't want to face the truth about myself because I wasn't ready to handle it. Second, my thinking was so rigid back then. I thought values had to be written in a certain way, maybe picked from a list, perfectly phrased as a noun or verb, something official. It felt overwhelming and too final; I was afraid that by writing them down, I'd be locking myself in and wouldn't be able to change my mind, so I didn't do it.

Years later, I finally took the time to define my values, and it changed everything. Our values express who we are. They don't have to follow any formula, we can write them as single words, short sentences, or even represent them with images, and they can change over time. They're ours. The important thing is to identify them.

Some of my core values are love, connection, security, helping people, authenticity, loyalty, simplicity, exploration, health, and self-growth. Knowing these values helps me make better choices, set healthy boundaries, and stay authentic. It also means I more naturally attract people who belong in my life, those who cheer me on, are honest with me, and help me grow.

But here's the thing: I don't like every value I have. Take security, for example. I sometimes wish it wasn't so high on my list because I believe it's kept me small at times, stopped me from taking reasonable risks, and maybe even robbed me of some joy. But I also see how it's saved me from trouble and helped me make solid, grounded decisions.

That's why I like to say we have to befriend our values. Accept them, understand how they serve us, and notice when they might be holding us back. With security, I know I'm naturally risk-averse. So when a big decision comes up, like buying a house, I trust my gut, knowing it has already run a built-in security check. And when a new opportunity appears, instead of shutting it down immediately, I give myself more time to think before answering because I know that my immediate response would probably be no.

When we know our values, we can use them as allies. *We can lean on them when they serve our goals, and work with them more mindfully when they get in the way.*

Today, I invite you to make a list of your top ten values. For each one, note whether it's a value you like or one that tends to cause you trouble. I encourage you to pick one that's challenging and brainstorm ways to "play nice" with it, so it works for you, not against you.

Daily Routine 37

1. Do the Heart to Yes technique.
2. Practice mindfulness meditation for ten minutes.
3. Journal for five to ten minutes.
4. Make a list of your top ten core values and rank them by importance. Identify the ones you like and the ones you don't and why. Here are a few tips:

- Each value can be expressed in its own way. Some will be one word, others a sentence or an image.
- Be as clear as possible and avoid perfectionism.
- Give yourself permission to refine them over time and even change them.
- Use somatic techniques to check how you feel about each value.

Layers of Identity

Although our core values tend to remain steady over time, other values can shift more easily. We can add new ones, remove some, and shape them over time. The same is true for our identity.

I believe identity is even more powerful than belief. It tends to feel more permanent and carry more weight in what we do. *Technically, identity can be described as a belief about who we are, and that belief powerfully shapes our actions.*

We don't just have one identity. We carry layers of them. That doesn't mean we're pretending to be different people, or living some kind of double life. It means we express different aspects of ourselves in different contexts.

Think about it. I'm Jean-François Moreau. I have certain values, health is one of them, so part of my identity is being an athlete. Connection and relationships are also deeply important to me, so I see myself as a faithful and caring partner, a loyal friend, and a loving father to my kids. These are all layers of my identity, and each one influences how I think, feel, and behave.

Naming these identities is powerful because our behavior naturally aligns with who we believe ourselves to be. If I want to train more, thinking of myself as an athlete makes it far easier to follow through. If I want to take better care of my relationships, seeing myself as a devoted father and loyal friend makes spending quality time with my kids and supporting my friends feel more natural.

Your task is to explore the identities you might want to try on. Be flexible. Some you may try and decide aren't for you and that's completely okay, you can let them go. Others you might choose to keep and grow into over time. Follow your gut, be honest with yourself, and most of all, have fun with it.

Trying on Other Identities

To try on new identities, I suggest two main approaches: the as-if game and self-hypnosis.

The as-if game is simple: you pretend to already be the identity you want to adopt. Let's say you want to try on the athlete identity. You might start reading about fitness, subscribing to podcasts or newsletters on training, or picking up a workout magazine. You'd surround yourself with health enthusiasts, connect with people at the gym, and start eating in a way that supports your athletic goals, all this *as-if* you were already living that identity.

And you've heard me say this before: there are no magic pills. If you want to be an athlete, you can't just sit on the couch all day. **We've got to be ready to do the work.**

That's where the second approach comes in: self-hypnosis. You can use it to boost motivation, using the first variation to simply let your unconscious mind take the lead: "I want to be motivated to go to the gym. I want to reinforce my identity as an athlete." Or you can guide the process yourself, using Timeline work to install the identity earlier in your life or to scan your future and remove the obstacles in your way. Those obstacles could be literal, like feeling low energy or symbolic, like big rocks in the road. Remove them, transform them, or send them off into the universe to release their energy. Your imagination is your only limit here, so do what works for you.

You can also use Ego State work in self-hypnosis, asking the different parts of yourself to help you step into this new identity and maintain it. Stick with an identity for a while to see how it feels. If it doesn't work, try another until you find one that feels authentic and beneficial to your life. And here's another tip: create an outfit that represents this identity. If you want to feel like an athlete, maybe it's a hockey uniform or running shoes. If you want to be an artist, maybe you put on a wig à la Bob Ross. When you need to be in that state, put on the outfit and let it shift how you feel.

Today, choose one identity you'd like to try on. Play the as-if game and support it with self-hypnosis. You can use Timeline work to plant this identity in your past and imagine a future where you are successfully embodying this identity. Or use Ego State work to enlist the help of different parts of yourself. You can even bring in a Visualization++ technique like Dress for Success to literally step into the identity. See how it feels, notice what changes, and have fun experimenting with who you can become.

Daily Routine 38

1. Do the Heart to Yes technique.
2. Practice mindfulness meditation for ten minutes.

3. Journal for five to ten minutes.
4. Try on a new identity. To help you, use Timeline and Ego State work with self-hypnosis. You can also use a Visualization++ technique such as the Dimmer Switch to intensify and empower your new identity.

Becoming the Real You

Being authentic takes so much courage, and you've already shown so much of it on this journey. I'm really proud of you. By being compassionate, honest with yourself, self-loving and by using the tools you've learned, you are developing authenticity and creating the life you deserve.

Being authentic is truly the best thing we can do for ourselves and for the people around us. *It doesn't mean we never change; it means staying true to our values while allowing room for flexibility.* Our non-core values can shift easily, our beliefs can evolve, and our behaviors can adapt.

When my marriage started falling apart, I had to take an honest look at my feelings for my ex, at myself, and at how I defined my identity. My identity was screaming for change. If I had refused to change at all, that would have been inauthentic. It takes courage to look at ourselves so closely, to be honest about what we find, and to embrace the changes authenticity demands of us. Sometimes, we discover parts of ourselves we didn't fully know before, and once we do, authenticity calls us to live in alignment with them.

This chapter has been all about getting closer to the real you by knowing your values, understanding the layers of your identity, and having the courage to try on new ones that serve you better. Authenticity isn't about being rigid; it's about staying true to what matters most while allowing space to grow, adapt, and evolve. Every tool you've explored in this book and practiced can help you shape the identity that feels most aligned with your deepest values. *And remember, identity is powerful because it shapes how you show up in the world. When you choose it with intention, you're not just becoming someone, you're becoming the real you.*

I believe in you.

Today, keep working on your beliefs and identity. Use the Transmuting Shape technique to strengthen an empowering belief, and bring in Ego State work to help you step fully into a useful identity. Let this be a day where you consciously shape who you are becoming, one choice at a time.

Daily Routine 39

1. Do the Heart to Yes technique.
2. Practice mindfulness meditation for ten minutes.
3. Journal for five to ten minutes.
4. Keep working on your beliefs and identity. Use the Transmuting Shape and Ego State work to help you adopt an empowering identity.

Our journey is almost complete. The next chapter will focus on staying motivated and setting you up for lasting success.

12. Staying Motivated and Long-Term Success

First of all, **congratulations!** You've made it through all forty days (or more) of this journey with me. That's no small feat. You committed to showing up each day, doing the work, and sticking with it until the end. Take a moment to truly celebrate that. You've accomplished something meaningful, and you've proven to yourself that you can follow through.

Now, the question is: how do you keep going? How do you take what you've learned here and make it a permanent part of your life?

The good news is that this entire journey has been designed to help you build strength, develop resilience, and give you a set of tools you can use for long-term success. You already have everything you need, you just need to keep using it.

One of the simplest ways to stay on track is to use hypnosis to reinforce your daily habits. You can go into trance for twenty minutes and simply tell your unconscious:

"Help me strengthen my daily habits, my Heart to Yes technique, my meditation, my journaling so that I naturally want to do them each day. When I open my eyes, I'll feel refreshed, motivated, and ready to act."

Beyond that, hold on to the structures that have supported you so far. Maintain your daily routine. Keep your daily reminders in place. If you don't yet have a partner to stay accountable with, find one. Even better, surround yourself with a community of people who are committed to growth, self-improvement, and living with intention.

If you're not already part of it, I invite you to join our community where we share wins, challenges, and insights (https://members.jftiger.com). Being around others who are walking the same path will keep you motivated and inspired.

Another powerful way to deepen your results is to go through the book again. The first time you experience new material, you absorb a certain amount. The second time, you catch things you missed before, and the repetition strengthens your practice. I once heard Jeffrey Allen say that repeating a training isn't just review, it's transformation at a deeper level. I couldn't agree more.

So set yourself up for success. Keep practicing what you've learned, keep refining your skills, and *keep showing up for yourself.* You've already proven you can do it. Now, let's make sure you keep building on that success for the rest of your life.

Coping with Setbacks and Challenges

Life has a way of throwing us curveballs. Impermanence is real, and sometimes our routines get disrupted. The important thing to remember is that we're not aiming for perfection, we're aiming for progress. Setbacks are part of the journey, and how we respond to them makes all the difference.

When you face a setback, the very first thing to give yourself is love, compassion, and gentleness. This isn't about judgment or beating yourself up, it's about seeing your routine as something fluid, a continuum, rather than all-or-nothing. Think of it like a dimmer switch. On one end, there's no routine at all, and on the other end, there's your ideal practice. Some days, the light will be bright and strong. Other days, you might only be able to turn it up a little.

Maybe one day all you have time for is five minutes of mindfulness and a quick Visualization++ exercise. That's okay. The next day, you might have more space to move the needle closer to your ideal routine. Over time, these adjustments build resilience rather than derail progress.

I've had my share of setbacks too. There were times it took me six months to get back into my healthy daily routine. It was frustrating, even disappointing. But here's what I learned: every time I came back, every time I started again, I felt the benefits almost immediately. And the more I practiced over the years, the easier it became to return after a break. The gaps between my practice grew smaller and smaller. And I believe the same will be true for you.

Even if your daily routine becomes shorter for a while, it can still make a meaningful difference in your life. Use the techniques as needed:

- Feeling nervous before a presentation? Try a quick self-hypnosis session or a Visualization++ exercise.
- Carrying a heavy, lingering emotion you can't quite understand? Do some journaling and see what emerges.
- Stuck in negative self-talk? Use the Heart to Yes technique to reframe it and connect to a better emotional state.
- Feeling emotionally tense or restless? Practice one of the somatic techniques—Chest Beating, Shaking, or Power Posing—to quickly shift your physiology.
- Needing clarity about a decision? Use the Timeline process to explore the potential future outcomes and find the choice that feels right for you.
- Lacking motivation or confidence? Do Ego State work to connect with the part of you that holds the resource you need.
- Want to reconnect to your goals? Revisit your values and identities, and empower them using your toolset to anchor your focus.

These are all tools you now have at your disposal. You don't need to use them all every day, just pick the one that fits your moment and needs.

And if you ever find yourself in a stretch where you can't do much, I want to share one final tip that has been a constant for me, even in the toughest times. It's something so simple, yet so powerful: gratitude.

When I wake up each morning, before I do anything else, I take a moment to be thankful. I thank life itself. I am grateful for my kids, my partner, the roof over my head, the food I have, and the opportunities ahead of me. I list as many things and people for which and whom I am grateful as I can think. Then I go a step further and express gratitude for the things I desire in the future, as if they're already in my life. This practice can take just one minute, but it shifts everything.

If you're struggling, let gratitude be your bare minimum. It will help you stay connected to what matters most, tune your mind to see and find what you want more of and gently bring you back toward your routine.

Recap and Staying Connected

And one last time, congratulations for completing this journey. I am so proud of you. To me, your greatest success is not just the fact that you reached the end, but that you have taken intentional, consistent care of yourself for the last forty days. That's no small thing. You've built a daily routine that empowers you and brings you back to your center. You've practiced the Heart to Yes technique, worked with your emotions and thoughts through mindfulness meditation and journaling, and explored the deeper layers of your inner world using powerful tools.

Over these weeks, you've learned how to process emotions in a healthy way, whether through somatic techniques, self-hypnosis, or Visualization++. You've challenged and released limiting beliefs, replacing them with empowering ones that support the life you want to create. You've explored who you are more deeply and experimented with new layers of identity, not to pretend to be someone else, but to refine the layers of who you already are so that your true self and worth shines through.

My encouragement to you now is to keep going. Keep up your daily routine, even if you need to adapt it to fit your life. Surround yourself with communities and people who believe in you, who will nudge you forward when you need it, and who will celebrate your wins alongside you. If you haven't already, please join our community at https://members.jftiger.com. My intention for this group is to create a safe space where we can share victories, offer support during struggles, and connect with others who are equally committed to growth and self-discovery.

Today marks the last day of our forty-day journey together, and this routine is designed to help you carry the momentum forward. Think of it as your launchpad into the next chapter of your life, a way to lock in the habits you've built, recharge your motivation, and remind yourself of the power you hold. You've done the work, learned the tools, and proven you can commit to yourself. Now, this routine will help you reinforce everything you've gained so you can continue creating success long after today.

Daily Routine 40

1. Do the Heart to Yes technique.
2. Practice mindfulness meditation for ten minutes.
3. Journal for five to ten minutes.
4. Use self-hypnosis with the method of your choice to strengthen your motivation and support long-term success.

Final Words

I wish you nothing but the best as you continue your journey toward greater authenticity, deeper self-discovery, and a richer, more intentional life. Thank you for walking this path with me. It has been a privilege to share what I've learned and what has helped me, and I believe these tools will serve you too. I believe in you. Now, believe in yourself. Go out there and live an amazing life.